Introverts in Love

The Quiet Way to Happily Ever After

Sophia Dembling

A Perigee Book

A PERIGEE BOOK
Published by the Penguin Group
Penguin Group (USA) LLC
375 Hudson Street, New York, New York 10014

USA • Canada • UK • Ireland • Australia • New Zealand • India • South Africa • China

penguin.com

A Penguin Random House Company

Library of Congress Cataloging-in-Publication Data

Dembling, Sophia.
Introverts in love : the quiet way to happily ever after / Sophia Dembling.— First edition.
pages cm
ISBN 978-0-399-17061-4 (paperback)
1. Introverts.   2. Interpersonal relations.   3. Dating (Social customs).   4. Courtship.
5. Man-woman relationships.   I. Title.
BF698.35.I59D457   2015
158.2—dc23   2014040023

First edition: January 2015

PRINTED IN THE UNITED STATES OF AMERICA

10 9 8 7 6 5 4 3 2 1

Text design by Laura K. Corless

Most Perigee books are available at special quantity discounts for bulk purchases for sales
promotions, premiums, fund-raising, or educational use. Special books, or book excerpts, can
also be created to fit specific needs. For details, write: Special.Markets@us.penguingroup.com.

To Tom, who likes that I don't talk much,
and yet reminds me to finish my sentences when necessary

Contents

x   Contents

Introduction

Why Introverts in Love

Love is complicated. It is both universal and highly individual. In a way, nobody is an expert on love, and in a way, everybody is. Love is the same for all of us; it must be, or songs about love wouldn't twang such universal chords. But it's also different—how often have you looked at a couple and wondered how they could possibly stay together?

Introversion and extroversion are only two small facets of all that makes us who we are. Each of us is a rich and complex slumgullion of traits and quirks, nature and nurture, hopes and dreams and irritating habits. And, of course, the most basic rules for relationship success are the same for introverts, extroverts, and everyone in between: Communication, compromise, respect. Same with things that lead to relationship failure. The details may change but the general principles are the same for everyone.

So if we know that, why a book just for and about introverts and love?

Well, for one thing, being an introvert can seem at odds with seeking and finding love. We just don't put ourselves out there as much as extroverts; and even when we do, we aren't as quick to make friends of strangers.

"I don't meet as many people as my friends because I generally prefer to stay home and delve into something really stimulating, like reading or video games," says Taylor, a 27-year-old single writer and an introvert. "I also don't tend to mingle too well with people at parties. I do better with friends there with me, and I can 'turn it on' and talk to just about anyone without awkwardness, but I often don't."

Not only that, but when introverts meet someone who sparks their interest, they often are uncomfortable making the first move of any kind. Ray-Mel, a 60-year-old artist and an introvert, says that he was so crushed the times he stepped out of his comfort zone and pursued someone only to be turned down, he decided it wasn't worth the risk. "After a while I just sat back and waited to be approached rather than do the approaching," he says. "That resulted in long inactive periods." (Fortunately, Ray-Mel met the perfect extrovert for him; you'll hear more about that later.)

On top of that, with our limited energy for interaction, where do we even find the juice for the search? How do we meet potential partners when mingling is such a chore for us? How do we stand out when we prefer to hold back?

And are introverts more likely to find love with an extrovert, who will bring sparkle and energy to our lives? Or an introvert, who will cozy up in quiet comfort with us?

You might never have asked yourself these questions explicitly, but they have affected your quest for love all the same.

And it doesn't end there. After we have found someone, our introversion comes into play in other ways. How do we let another person into our hearts while still honoring the introversion that makes us private people? How do we balance the togetherness we want and the solitude we need without hurt feelings and misunderstandings? How many phone calls and text messages every day are too many?

For a lot of people, a new love interest is all consuming, but even a new love interest can't trump a need for solitude for some introverts. John, a 59-year-old divorced engineer, wonders about the challenge of "maintaining confidence in his introversion and independence in a society that pushes the concept of relationship dependence." Drew, a 34-year-old single attorney, says that inevitably any woman he dates will eventually complain that she is not getting enough time from him. "How much time do you need?" he wonders. "Daily? I can't do that." Is it possible some people aren't cut out for full-time relationships? I'll talk about that, too.

Throughout this book you'll find interviews with introverts—single, coupled, divorced, straight and gay, and even one who identifies as polyamorous—who told me about looking for and finding romantic partners, about their relationships, good and strained, about what they have and what they want, why they are happy and how they could be happier. I talked to introverts in relationships with extroverts and introverts in relationships with other introverts. I talked to newlyweds and to people who had been married for many years.

Why didn't I talk to extroverts, too? Well, I think we've already heard a lot from extroverts, whether from the extroverts we know or the extroverts who have, until recently, tended to dominate public conversation. After all, speaking up is one of the things extroverts do best.

Besides, one thing I've learned since I started writing about introversion in 2009 is that a lot of introverts out there didn't know they were introverts until they started reading about it and hearing what other introverts have to say. All they knew was that they felt like weirdos, and that people were always telling them they were doing life wrong and should be different.

In the years since, introversion has become a hot topic; introverts have been gleefully surfing a learning curve, figuring out who they are and how they function in the world. My first book, *The Introvert's Way: Living a Quiet Life in a Noisy World*, was a general guide to life as an introvert, and I heard from many, many introverts that it helped them recognize, accept, and articulate their own needs. Now I hope to do the same with introverts and relationships. While I will discuss mistakes introverts can make in their relationships with extroverts, this book is for introverts and about introverts. Extroverts are invited to read it, of course, but you won't hear their voices in these pages.

Some of what we discuss here may have you nodding in agree-
ment, some may shed new light on an aspect of yourself or your
relationship, some may leave you with question marks floating
around your head. That's OK. As with any advice, you take what
fits and forget the rest. The purpose of this book is not to provide
a no-fail formula for happy relationships (if only I could, I would
be so rich!) but to suggest some things to consider in your own
pursuit of happily ever after.

If you're in the process of looking for love, I hope this book will
help you identify qualities that sound compatible with your particular style of introversion. I also hope this book will help you
open up explicit discussions about what you need as an introvert,
and will make this discussion easier by showing you that others
share your feelings and how they handle them. Here is a road map
for talking about needing solitude even in the context of intimate relationships; about socializing versus staying home; about
how we handle conflict. Knowing that your feelings about these
things are 100 percent A-OK and shared by others will, I hope,
give you confidence in weeding out of your life those people who
try to change or shame you.

If you are in a relationship, you might have already worked
through many of the issues discussed here—or maybe not. If not,
perhaps something here will give you a different perspective on a
recurring problem or discomfort, be it morning chatter or guilt
trips over your need for occasional time away.

My goal here is not to present definitive answers as much as shed light on various relevant issues that may arise. And the wonderful thing is that if you are in a relationship with open communication and mutual respect, issues once identified can be worked out. And that's how you get on, and stay on, the road to happily ever after.

PART I

To Get There, You Have to Know Where You're Going

What Do You Want from a Relationship?

Birds of a Feather,
or Opposites Attract?

Should You Seek
an Introvert or an Extrovert?

The question I'm asked more than any other when it comes to relationships is: Are introvert-introvert unions best because they understand each other's ways? Or are introvert-extrovert couples happier because they balance each other out?

The unsatisfying answer is yes.

Yes, birds of a feather flock together, and yes, opposites attract. It just depends.

"It was stressful being married to an extrovert," says Tone, a 43-year-old pensioner. "We never had the same needs for a social life and I had to push myself every day trying to meet my ex's need for being around people and doing the things that he thought the both of us should do."

Now Tone is married to an introvert and says it's a big relief. "He understands my needs and how I think because he feels the same. I feel peaceful inside for the first time in my life."

However, Tyler, a 28-year-old church technical director, found dating an introverted woman difficult. "When I'm in a crowd or social situation, it's pretty much everything I can do to maintain what I'm doing. I couldn't really babysit someone who wasn't able to handle the situation. I can do one or the other, that's it."

The woman he ultimately married about five years ago "can make friends with a rock," he says, and that's part of what attracted him to her. "I was really surprised at how many friends she had and how much energy she put into spending time with those friends," he says. "I guess I kind of admired it."

The introverts I talked to who were in relationships are almost evenly divided between introvert-introvert couples and introvert-extrovert couples. And the few divorced introverts I spoke to are also equally divided—some divorced from introverts, some from extroverts.

So, where does this leave us? In the fuzzy gray "it depends" area between birds of a feather and opposites attract. Because, as it turns out, introversion and extroversion may not even come into play when it comes to the kind of people who attract us. Research by psychologist Glenn Geher suggests that we choose partners who resemble our opposite-sex parent, although the personality trait of extroversion (which is what psychologists measure—by their definition, introverts are people who are low on extroversion) is not a big player in either our choice of mates or our marital happiness. The traits of agreeableness and neuroticism appear to be more important.

Dr. Helen Fisher has also found no connection between introversion/extroversion and relationship success. A biological anthropologist who has made a career studying the chemistry of romantic attachment, Fisher is the brain behind the questionnaire used by online dating site Chemistry.com. In her book, *Why Him? Why Her?: How to Find and Keep Lasting Love*, she explains her research into behavior, attraction, and brain chemistry—specifically the amounts and activity of dopamine, serotonin, testosterone, and estrogen.

Fisher says various cocktails of these chemicals create four personality types that are the basis of attraction. To oversimplify her findings, the laws of attraction, she says, boil down to four broad, biologically triggered personality types: the Explorer (impulsive and adventurous, among other things); the Builder (traditional and family oriented); the Director (logical and analytical); and the Negotiator (imaginative and intuitive).

Introversion and extroversion aren't mentioned in the descriptions of these four types. "This aspect of personality doesn't play a decisive role in our romantic attractions," Fisher writes. (Note that she says *decisive* role; it may play some role, and you get to choose whether it's a bit part or a major player.) It seems possible that introverts whose dominant trait is Explorer will be drawn to extroverts, who will drag them out of their comfort zone, while Builder introverts are likely to be attracted to other Builders, who will be happy to hunker down at home with them.

Both types of relationships have their risks and benefits. Introverts can find themselves constantly fighting for the space they need if they connect with an extrovert who doesn't get it. That's the sort of thing that contributed to the breakdown of John's marriage.

"There was never an understanding from my wife about why I was the way I was, why I would find a quiet corner and isolate myself during a party, or why sometimes I would withdraw from her when she was in her 'pay attention to me!' moods," he says. Though John tried to explain, and even recommended books, she continued to feel hurt and unloved, he continued to feel stressed, and the whole thing fell apart.

Introvert-introvert couples have their challenges, too. Many of the introverts I spoke to admitted to being nonconfrontational, which has drawbacks. If two introverts are particularly passive or overthinkers, as introverts often are, they might get stuck in a weird state of suspended animation. Paul, a 46-year-old architectural designer, and his girlfriend of twenty years both find making decisions stressful and so, he says, "So much is left undone. Twenty years together and still not married. I think our introversion has a lot to do with it."

And there's always the risk of two introverts indulging in isolation more than is good for one or both of them. My husband and I are both introverts, though he less so than I. He deals with people all day at work while I work alone. At the end of the day, he's ready for quiet home time, and although I might crave some socializing, it's so much easier for me to just hit the couch with him. Staying home is always my default and sometimes I wish one of us were a little more extroverted, to help motivate us both.

Not that there's anything wrong with being homebodies if that's what feels right. Ed, a 45-year-old student in environmental biology, and Rebecca, a 46-year-old graphic and fine artist, are introverts and have been married since 2012. They're perfectly happy hermits. "We enjoy living out in the country where it would take effort for friends and family to come, discouraging unannounced visits," Ed says. "I get most of my social needs met at school, she at work, and both of us via social networking."

So the bottom line is that there is no right or wrong, no magic formula when it comes to introverts and love. We all have different needs, and the best thing we can do is recognize and respect our own personal needs, strengths, and weaknesses, and find the partner who clicks with those.

In his book *Personal Intelligence: The Power of Personality and How It Shapes Our Lives*, John D. Mayer writes, "Whether we are trying to fit ourselves into a relationship or a career, it's not like fitting a plug into a socket—we are more multifaceted than that. It's more like fitting a tuba into a duffel bag." Our personalities have all kinds of shapes and angles and fiddly bits, but with a little effort and finesse, the bag can accommodate all of it.

Cupid's arrow goes where it goes and nobody can predict with certainty whose heart it will pierce. But as an introvert, if you're not already in a relationship, it can't hurt to give a little thought to whether you would prefer someone to draw you out or come into your cave with you. And if you're already in a relationship, this book might help you notice and appreciate (or adjust if necessary) the intersection of your introversion with your partner's personality. While your introversion isn't the be-all and end-all of who you are, it is an important trait and, for many of us, one that is only just finding a voice.

Five Reasons Why
Introverts Are Where It's At

Why would you want to spend your life with an introvert? Here are a few reasons to consider:

1. They get it. More than anything, many introverts are tremendously relieved to find another soul who understands the pleasure of quiet, a restrained social life, home, and tranquility. "We like the same things and love to spend time at home, living the quiet life," says Tone. "I appreciate that she understands the benefits and the need for having this quiet space in the day," says Doug M., a 32-year-old writer and newlywed.

It can be a tremendous relief to be with someone who doesn't lay on guilt trips when you need a little bit of space to be with your own thoughts. Another introvert gets introversion fully and completely without any complicated or awkward explanations.

2. The sweet sound of silence. Introverts don't chatter. "We spend a lot of time just sitting with each other not talking," says Julie, a 22-year-old marketing professional who lives with her introverted boyfriend.

An introvert is a lot less likely than an extrovert to fuss if you're being quiet or if you need some time inside your own head, with your computer, video games, books, or whatever you like to lose yourself in. Introverts don't keep a running commentary going about life (except in their heads, but you don't have to listen to that) and understand that you can feel close and connected with another person even in silence. And introverts get that morning is not the time for nattering, and that after a hard day at work, some time to unwind is mighty nice. An extra plus: Getting away, physically, from your partner isn't nearly as pressing when you can be in close proximity without having to actually interact. It's the next best thing to being alone.

3. No party pressure. "We like to go out and do things together, but don't really enjoy large crowds or having to interact with a lot of people," says Rebecca. "So if one of us says they would rather not go to a particular event, the other rarely minds."

Introverts are often relieved when plans cancel, so with another introvert, you can usually back out of social obligations with no repercussions. Knowing that you both enjoy, or dislike, the same sorts of things means that deciding which invitations to accept and which to decline requires minimal negotiation, and even when you decide to show up, chances are good you'll be ready to leave at about the same time. (Unless you happen to be married to someone even more introverted than you, like Arden, a 51-year-old business etiquette consultant. "He would prefer to stay home and putz around the house," she says. "I want to go out to dinner, see a movie or play, travel, see friends, et cetera.")

4. They won't try to drag you onto the dance floor. And I mean that both literally and figuratively. Another introvert is not likely to lay the whole "try it, you'll like it" trip on you if you already know you won't like it, whatever it is: Karaoke, the bunny hop, skinny-dipping with the gang. Another introvert will find it a lot easier to take no for an answer and you won't have to justify your preferences.

Of course, the chances of any introvert trying to drag you into that kind of thing are slim, but should it happen, another introvert is much more likely to understand and accept your reluctance than an extrovert, who might try to persuade you that it will be good for you or it's healthy to step out of your comfort zone. Yes, it's healthy to step out of your comfort zone, but less so to be dragged out of it kicking and screaming.

5. A companion for introvert fun. What's your idea of a really good time? Curling up on the couch with a book? Hiking a quiet trail? An art museum and a sidewalk café? A long road trip? While of course you can enjoy these things alone, wouldn't it be nice to have an equally happy, warm body next to you on the couch? To have someone's hand to hold when you reach a beautiful view?

Someone who will let you view art in silence but talk about it after? Someone who is OK letting the road unspool in companionable silence, but also enjoys discussing the kinds of deep thoughts that bubble up on a road trip?

I don't suggest extroverts don't enjoy these things, because I know they do, but their appetite for them will be more quickly sated and then they're ready to get social. They need to get social. "As much as we do enjoy being with other people, we definitely enjoy just the two of us the most," says Nancy, a 59-year-old graphic artist married to an extrovert. "But two or three days of just the two of us is enough for Susan."

Five Reasons Why
Extroverts Are Great to Date

Introverts and extroverts can be wonderfully compatible. Here are a few reasons why:

1. Fun on the extrovert ride. "I absolutely love, love, love being around people who are very fun and gregarious and say 'let's go here, let's go there,'" says Laura, a 50-ish nutritionist and media professional whose main squeeze is an extrovert.

Many introverts have the spirit of adventure but not a lot of *oomph* when it comes to making stuff happen. Extroverts have ideas, they have energy, and they have a strong desire to get out and do stuff, preferably around people.

Obviously, this won't sound good to all introverts; there are some who can't imagine why anyone would want to go to a party. But other introverts do want to join the fun, in their own way, and having an extrovert around to get the party going is the best of both worlds: All the fun with almost none of the effort. Just hang on and enjoy.

2. You won't want for friends. I hear it from introverts often and have felt it myself: Making friends is difficult, especially for those of us who don't do casual conversation easily, prefer not to be around large groups, and tend to get quiet in a crowd. And it's not that we don't want friends, it's just not easy to make new ones.

Extroverts, however, are experts at meeting and connecting with new people, and if your partner has that gift, you can benefit, too. "Even before I was married, one of my best friends was a *huge* extrovert," says Chris, a 45-year-old Web services director. "I seem to like having an extrovert in my life to help pull me out of my shell and help me make friends."

3. No guessing games. Extroverts enjoy articulating the thoughts that cross their minds. Possibly every thought that crosses their minds, which can be wearing at some times and a huge relief at others. If an extrovert wants something or is upset or angry about something, out it comes, *boom*, right there to deal with. They don't let things build up like many introverts will (you know who you are).

Many ultra-sensitive introverts have little mood radars constantly circulating, looking for cues and clues to others' state of mind. When we pick something up, it goes into our brains to be cranked around and around and around as we try to extract whatever relevant meaning it might hold for us and the state of our relationship. As well as being absolutely exhausting, this can be counterproductive. Even the most sensitive people tend to be pretty bad at mind reading (as in, really terrible at mind reading—as in, can't mind read at all, it's impossible, forget about it), and all that thinking and guessing and ruminating—because that's what it is—doesn't do a relationship any good.

But you don't have to drag things out of extroverts. And once they've had their say, they're ready to move on. "We're both pretty easygoing but I can get pretty swelled up and stay that way for a while," says Ray-Mel, who has been married to an extrovert for twenty-five years. "If she gets mad at me about something, she'll have her rant about it, but she's better than me about dropping things."

4. Action! "If phone calls need to be made, I sit and think about it," says David, a 50-year-old life coach who has been married to an extrovert for six years. "She just does it."

Indeed. Navel-gazing is an introvert hobby, and while it is great to be a deep thinker full of insight and analysis, sometimes we can get so involved in looking at all sides of the issue that we paralyze ourselves. (First drafts of many things I write often have copious use of the phrase "on the other hand." So many hands, they can only get in each other's way.)

Extroverts, on the other hand, are action oriented, far less likely to measure the repercussions of their every move. Whether this is always the best approach to life is debatable (let's sit and think about that for a while), but it can jolt us out of overthinking ruts and get things moving.

Granted, the flip side of that is that extroverts might get started on something but if something else comes along that needs to be done, might then flit off to the next thing, leaving you to finish up. But that's where the next benefit of dating an extrovert comes into play . . .

5. That yin-yang thing. Look at it this way: There are two parts to accomplishing anything. The first is thinking about what needs to be done, the second is doing it. Beautiful music is made of major and minor chords. Sunny days and gray days both have their charms.

Introvert and extrovert. We complement each other.

The extrovert can get you out and about and show you how to work a room and then, when the party's over, you can teach the extrovert how to relax and unwind. "My girlfriend often remarks how much of a calming influence I give her," says Robert, a 58-year-old librarian. "And I learn some social skills from her, which may be handy."

An extrovert can get you out of the house for some outdoor fun, you can help the extrovert pause and notice how the trees look against the blue of the sky. An extrovert can get things out on the table for discussion, you can bring analysis and nuance to the discussion (after you've had time to think about it, but more on that later). An extrovert can help make sure you have a life outside the house, you can ensure that home is a welcoming place when the party is over.

Yes, there are definitely some benefits to opposites attracting, if that's what works for you.

Extroverts Sparkle, Introverts Glow

What You Bring to the Dating Game

My best friend in high school was a pretty, outgoing, talkative extrovert. Not only did she have gorgeous skin, a cute figure, and shiny brown hair that fell practically to her bottom, she also was flirtatious, opinionated, and quick to laugh. Boys were irresistibly drawn to her, and it seemed to me that she could get the adoring attention of anyone she wanted. At parties, she was the center of attention, the one laughing the loudest and flirting the hardest, and enrapturing everyone she met. In social situations I felt dumpy, clumsy, and dull next to her.

About four hundred years later, when through the modern miracle of the Internet I reconnected with people from high school, I was dumbfounded to learn that I hadn't been nearly as invisible as I'd thought. People noticed me, boys noticed me, even one of my secret crushes noticed me and admitted that he'd had a little crush on me, too. (Too bad neither of us said anything at the time, but that's high school.)

This realization forced me to recast my whole high school experience and, to an extent, my own self-image, in a different light. A softer one.

Here's the point: Sometimes we imagine that to get attention, we have to compete with extroverts' glitter and sparkle, and that can be discouraging. But it's also not correct. Remember how your mom used to tell you that if you just be yourself, the right person will come along? For what is probably not the first time, your mother was right.

The reality is that you are not competing with extroverts for attention. Extroverts and introverts are apples and oranges. Extroverts sparkle, introverts glow. Extroverts are fireworks, introverts are a fire in the hearth. Extroverts attract people who like razzle-dazzle, introverts attract people who want to bask in your warmth.

Remember that, if you're looking for a one and only.

If you come from a family where introversion was not appreciated (or even if you didn't), you might set out on your quest for the right relationship with a one-down mind-set, imagining you will be easily overlooked or will have to behave like someone you're not in order to get attention. But that's not the way to go. People are drawn to others who are comfortable in their own skin, which means knowing yourself and liking who you are.

Besides, trying to be who you aren't in order to attract a mate can backfire in so many ways. First of all, there's a matter of truth in advertising. My husband still brings up the very sexy top I wore to the party where he finally asked me out. "I never saw it again," he says, with a hint of wry bitterness. It was the first and only time I ever wore that thing. It just wasn't me. It was a blouse for an exhibitionist, not an introvert. While Tom has forgiven the deception (sort of), it offers a lesson: Don't misrepresent yourself or, even if everything else works out, you'll never hear the end of it.

But even if you don't dress like Beyoncé when you're more Adele, if you kick your extrovert side into high gear to attract someone and then, when you're all comfy cozy together, reveal yourself as the introvert you are, you've done both of you a disservice. You may have gotten involved with someone who would prefer to be involved with an extrovert, which does not portend well for happily ever after. After a while, you might find yourself resenting their expectation that the party will go on forever, while they might feel like they've been hoodwinked into an ill-fitting relationship. (College students, take note: These are the days when it's easy to fake extroversion because there's always a party. Things change out in the real world when parties don't come to you and you have to make an effort.)

I remember incidents in my youth when I tried to emulate my extroverted best friend. Most of the time they ended with me feeling foolish or getting the kind of attention I didn't like.

I didn't have a boyfriend in high school in part because I didn't know what I had to offer. My high school friend knew exactly what drew people to her. They liked her flirtatiousness. They liked her bubbliness. They liked her audacious in-your-faceness. But at that time, I had no idea what people might like in me. I was smart but remember complaining, "Nobody ever says, 'Holy cow! Look at the IQ on that girl!'" My friends found me funny, but I was more about the witty aside than regaling the masses. I was a good sounding board, but, like most introverts, I was selective about close friends so most people didn't benefit from that.

I wish I'd been more like Niza, currently a junior in high school. "People seem to be drawn to my personality and awkwardness," she says. "Strangely, my introversion works for me, which is cool!"

Cool indeed.

Of course, many (most?) people reading this book are long past high school, but insecurity knows no age. I've heard from many, many adults over the years who admit that they did not appreciate—were even ashamed of—their own introversion before the "introvert-positive" movement got rolling in recent years.

To an extent, dating requires doing a sort of sales job on yourself. But you can't do a good job of that unless you believe in your product and know its best features. While of course you have individual wonderfulness that is part of your own personal sales pitch, you also bring some fine qualities into relationships that are partly a function of your introversion. For example, my husband doesn't have patience for yakety-yakkers and appreciates that I'm not a big talker. I'm also pretty low maintenance; I don't need or want 24/7 attention.

So, for your consideration, some of introverts' best features:

I hear you: Several introverts cited listening skills as among our best attributes. "I really try to understand and process what the other person is saying and where they are coming from before I respond," says Kristen, a 30-year-old client services rep and a newlywed. "I generally think carefully before I say something, especially something of a serious nature. Not to say I *never* blurt out stupid or hurtful things—who doesn't?—but it's less likely, I hope."

And I don't shoot from the hip: Similarly, Lynne says, "I like to have time to process the situation and then decide how best to respond. This can be helpful, as words spoken cannot be retracted or forgotten easily, or at all." And David thinks his marriage to an extrovert benefits from his ability to pause and reflect, "taking time, instead of rushing headlong into something."

Deep thoughts: This slow thoughtfulness means that introverts bring depth to relationships by digging into ideas and thinking things through thoroughly. We take the time to know the people we care about. "I like to learn everything about a person I'm dating, and I try to be as open and communicative as possible," says Taylor, adding, "I'm extremely loyal and reliable." And Melissa points out that a preference for quality one-on-one time takes relationships to deeper levels than they might otherwise reach.

I'll let you shine: Introverts also know when to step back and let others do their thing. Laura, who prefers dating extroverts, says she is fine letting her extrovert have center stage, which, she says, "feeds their need and they don't feel threatened." And, she says, "I also love riding along on the adventure path of an extrovert . . . basking in that energy but not having to worry about planning and more. So I have been told I am a great travel partner for my boyfriends!"

Indeed. And while extroverts can forge an adventure path and help introverts socialize or come out of their shells (or the house), introverts bring flip-side benefits to extroverts.

And provide a quiet space to recharge: "My husband is a high-energy extrovert who works in sales and also is energized by getting involved in politics, which I tolerate when I have to for his sake, but personally find draining," says Kristen. "After all the pushing and shouting in both of these areas, it's nice to come home to a peaceful home environment to unwind."

"I like to think I bring a core of quietness, a home hearth to our relationship," says Robert.

I get things done the introvert's way: And Doug H., an analytical engineer ("A group of engineers other engineers call geeks," he says) who also plays the trombone, met his extroverted wife at Ohio State University, which has a famous marching band. "They're very physical, and if you don't know how to march their way, there's essentially no way you can make it," Doug says. (Look for them on YouTube; you'll see what he means.) He tried out for the band as a freshman and was cut, "like half the people that tried out." Then, rather than griping and bad-mouthing the band, as his now-wife had heard others do, he hunkered down to study the way the band marched, he practiced, and he made the cut his sophomore year—impressing her with his solid introvert traits of tenacity and quiet determination. Later on, after they were married and when they had hit a rough patch, Doug brought that same sort of low-key resoluteness to their problems, researching and reading up on relationships in order to learn what he needed to know for a happy marriage. Which is introverted, geeky, and wonderful, and surely contributed to his long marriage.

Introverts have many stellar qualities that we play close to the chest. But if you can't see them in yourself, you can't expect others to see them.

What are your finest qualities?

Loving the One You're With?
Or Choosing the One You Love?

How Going with the Flow Can
Get You into the Wrong Relationship

Are you looking for love or waiting for love to find you?

If you're a quiet introvert who prefers sitting in the corner, and if you're accustomed to feeling like you're always overlooked, having the high beams of an extrovert's attention turned on you can be flattering, if not blinding. It's hard not to be drawn in when the center of attention wants to share the spotlight with you, and it's hard to resist a forceful personality reaching out and pulling you in.

On one hand, this is fine. Many introverts are not comfortable being the pursuer in relationships. Dan, a 44-year-old computer tech who married an extrovert he met on the job, says, "Given that I was/am also shy with women, dating an introverted woman would have been difficult and long. Actually the dating wouldn't have been bad; getting around to asking her out would have been long and difficult."

Ray-Mel, who was first pursued by his wife, says, "I think some-one who approaches someone else is by nature extroverted. . . . Recovering from a rejection isn't as difficult as it is for someone who is more introverted and finds it hard enough to make an approach at all."

There's absolutely nothing wrong with recognizing you're not the pursuer type. It's the kind of self-knowledge that can put you on the path to a happy ending. Many of the introverts I spoke to said that they did tend to be the pursued rather than the pursuer, but some also realized that it meant they didn't always make conscious choices in their relationships. "I'm very shy and too afraid of embarrassment to put myself out there," says 17-year-old Niza. And so even though she's not interested in super-friendly guys who have lots and lots of friends everywhere, she usually ends up with talkative extroverts. "Which is probably why we didn't work out," she says. "I always get bored or aggravated with the person and dump him."

Because of our tendency to let others take the lead, we are at risk of being sucked into relationships we might not have chosen if we'd given it more thought.

We've already talked about why introverts can be appealing to extroverts: We let them have the spotlight, we listen to them, and the rapt attention we are capable of providing (or at least faking) is irresistible to an attention-hungry extrovert. And some extroverts genuinely need us (whether or not they're aware of it) to help them slow down sometimes. "It's easy for her to get pulled a thousand ways by people," says Nancy about her "large-and-in-charge" wife.

"To have someone who can be quiet with her is really a healthy thing for her."

All this is 100 percent A-OK. If you find nourishment in the energy of an extrovert, if you enjoy basking in a reflected spotlight, if you are endlessly entertained by extroverted antics, or any of the other myriad reasons you might be drawn to extroverts, then let that extrovert woo you and enjoy.

All I suggest is that if you are going to be drawn into an extrovert's whirl, be sure you do it consciously and for the right reasons. Don't just fall in love with someone loving you, if you know what I mean. Actually, that's probably good advice for anyone, introvert or extrovert. But because introverts are less likely to stick their necks out to make connections, we can be more easily drawn into an extrovert's attention without considering whether it's the kind of attention that feeds our souls.

Among the risks of letting the extrovert choose you is that after the initial thrill of your undivided attention wanes, the extrovert might wait for something more exciting to happen, leading to hurtful disappointment. Or you might learn that you enjoy all that fuss and bother only to a degree and after a while find yourself wondering irritably why this bundle of noise and energy doesn't just calm down and read a book or something. (Granted, you might grumble about that sometimes even if the relationship is generally successful. Just as your extrovert might sometimes wish you would put out a little more energy around people. No relationship is without frustrations, and that's fine, if they're fleeting.) You might tire of sharing your loved one with his or her three hundred closest friends.

You might get tired of being dragged to parties, or your extrovert might get tired of having to be the engine of your mutual social life.

You might even find you feel threatened by your outgoing extrovert's easy charms with strangers. In an online essay, "6 Things Every Extrovert Secretly Has to Deal With," extroverted writer Macy Santo Domingo complains that "people will often assume you're flirting," even when you are just being your ordinary, outgoing extroverted self. This is a problem for her, she continues, when her friendliness is "misinterpreted as something more, especially when the person you are talking to gets offended that you are not, in fact, hitting on them."

Some extroverts might have a flirtatious manner that they have trouble turning off whether or not they intend to flirt. While this might be a little irritating for the extrovert, it can feel deeply threatening for an introverted partner who perceives flirtation and its attendant attention differently.

Of course, you also have to trust your gut because while it could be your extrovert is just being friendly, it also could be genuine flirtation. If it is flirtatiousness, use your gut again to determine whether it's all in fun or an actual threat. And regardless of whether it's a genuine threat or not, if you dislike it and the extrovert is unwilling to ratchet it back for your peace of mind, then you get to decide if you're OK with this in your relationship.

If any of these relationship breakdowns happen, it's important to remind yourself that it's just part of finding your way to love. An extrovert might choose you, but you always have the option to opt out if the fit is wrong. If the extrovert you were dating ultimately found you dull, don't take his or her word for it without first asking yourself what this person's criteria for "interesting" are. They might be entirely different from your own, and entirely different from the person you want to be. In other words, you're not dull just because this person thinks you are.

Actually, the person might be reacting to something that has little to do with you. My friend Carol Lennox, LPC, a therapist in Austin, Texas, points out that problems in the relationship often trace back to childhood stuff. An extrovert who was neglected as a child might be drawn to introverts because that lack of attention feels familiar, she says. "This hooks into the childhood pain and makes them angry at the introvert, who may be simply being themselves."

In his classic self-help book, *Getting the Love You Want: A Guide for Couples*, Harville Hendrix points out that most of us look for mates who are like the people who raised us, in order to do it right this time. "Our old brain . . . is trying to recreate the environment of childhood. And the reason the old brain is trying to resurrect the past is not a matter of habit or blind compulsion but of a compelling need to heal old childhood wounds."

In that case, by choosing you, the other person may be subconsciously opting in to a relationship that has problems built right into it from the get-go. And you may or may not be doing the same thing, depending on whether you are genuinely attracted to the relationship or if you just allowed yourself to get sucked into it.

Sound like pretty heavy stuff? Well, there's not a lot in the world that's heavier than choosing the person with whom we feel safe to be ourselves, which is one good reason to wait until we have a reasonably mature view of our needs and wants before we set our life/love path. Getting to know oneself that well can be a long and difficult process, often learned through a lot of trial and error, which in relationships can also mean an awful lot of hurt.

If you frequently find yourself in relationships with friends or lovers who make you feel small and less than, or if you find yourself frequently exhausted in a relationship from the effort of maintaining a persona the other person expects, maybe you're letting others choose you rather than choosing to be with people who make you feel wonderful. It might be time to step back and think a little bit: What do you want in a relationship, and is that what you are finding? Are you settling for not-quite-right relationships because they find you?

Get Out of Your Way

Ways We Might Let
Our Introversion Trip Us Up

Whether we're trying to find friends or lovers, we introverts don't always act in our own best interest.

For example, at one point I found myself feeling lonely, and this puzzled me. I get a lot of invitations to stuff, especially on Facebook. I'm frequently invited to parties and club events, to art happenings and networking events, and all sorts of more-the-merrier gatherings. Some I attend, many I don't. With all those invitations, I wondered, why did I feel lonely? The reason for this suddenly hit me: A lot of invitations are for extroverted events. After all, which people are most likely to extend invitations? Extroverts. And those invitations are very likely to be for extrovert-friendly activities.

If you're looking for love, I do recommend saying yes to as many invitations as sound even remotely interesting, to put yourself in the proximity of other interesting people. But I also know that after a while you might find yourself getting exhausted, or feeling increasingly reluctant, until finally "no, thanks" is just a whole lot easier. And that's when you might, like I did, start feeling isolated.

The introvert's dilemma is that we might not get a lot of invitations for the kind of socializing we like best—small, mellow gatherings. In other words, the kind of socializing other introverts like to do. Because, let's face it: We're introverts. We're all at home waiting to be invited to do introvert things. Which means, of course, that none of us are getting the invitations we crave. It's an introvert standoff.

If you don't have any introverted besties with whom casual get-togethers, or even not-so-casual get-togethers, are easy, finding introvertish people can be challenging. Do you see the catch-22? If you're looking for an introvert, then you want to meet people who are perfectly happy hanging out alone. And so there we sit in our rooms, waiting for an invitation that sounds just right to drift over the transom.

Except, bummer . . . it doesn't happen like that. Unless you put some effort into nurturing specific relationships—relationships that might not be the easiest ones to develop with people who might not be easy to find—the invitations most likely to materialize are from people who invite everyone to the party.

It's a predicament that only we can solve for ourselves. And that means putting on our big girl (or boy) pants and reaching out to likely suspects. Try throwing your own little get-togethers and inviting people you might not know that well yet but would like to. Maybe you could start a book club (more on that later). Or get in touch with that person with whom you exchange frequent never-kept promises to have lunch "sometime." Sooner or later "sometime" has to be now.

I'm not suggesting this is easy. First, it requires motivation. Then it requires gumption. Then it requires getting over any self-consciousness. Then it requires actually making contact.

The trouble with introvertish invitations, as opposed to extroverty invitations, is that they are a lot more intimate. They are not broadcast far and wide via Facebook, and this can make them scary. Small gatherings can make you feel vulnerable and have the potential to go all awkward on you. But if you never take the risk, never put yourself out there, then you exponentially decrease your chances of meeting potential partners.

Another way introverts can get in our own way is by staying too defended in our introvert bubble. "Somebody has to practically fall at my feet and say 'I am interested in you' or I don't notice them," Laura says. "I walk around with blinders. I am not an extrovert when I walk into a room. If I walk into a restaurant, I focus on the table, on the person I'm with."

Laura is not insecure. She's an attractive media professional who takes pains with her appearance, but she sometimes feels overwhelmed by the attention men pay her. While not all of us have this particular problem, many of us do keep those introvert blinders on a little too much. This isn't a bad strategy for avoiding that overwhelmed feeling when we first enter a situation, but if you never take off the blinders—if you never look around, look up from your book, make eye contact, or in any other way open yourself up to the people around you—then you might be missing out on all kinds of wonderful.

We also sometimes indulge our introversion too deeply by keeping so much to ourselves that other people have no chance to appreciate who we are. I don't suggest you have to put yourself all up in other people's faces, but you don't want to make people work too hard to know and like you. Taylor says, "I feel like the filter in my brain is too heavy. Nearly everything that goes through my head is gone so fast, I feel like there's no reason to bring it up. I think way too much about what I want to say and simply edit myself into silence."

I absolutely know what he means—I have been known to let sentences trail off in the middle because what I'm saying suddenly seems unnecessary. But this isn't particularly helpful when you're trying to connect with people. If you have to work too hard to be heard, then maybe you're not with the right people or person, but if you let opportunities to speak up slide by, then you are not giving others a chance to know you, or yourself a chance to show what you have.

Taylor also says that although he will pursue women, "I have to be extremely interested." And, he adds, "I guess I'm very picky in the sense that I don't really actively pursue unless I have some indication that they're interested. Rejection is scary, ya know?"

I do know. It is. And protecting yourself is not unwise. But if you're so fearful of rejection that you allow possibilities to pass you by, then you are placing shackles on your own freedom to choose, to acquire what you desire.

In one of my favorite self-helpy books, *The Consolations of Philosophy*, Alain de Botton writes that we seem afflicted by the need to "listen to everyone, to be upset by every unkind word and sarcastic observation. We fail to ask ourselves the cardinal and most consoling question: on what basis has this dark censure been made? We treat with equal seriousness the objections of the critic who has thought rigorously and honestly and those of the critic who has acted out of misanthropy or envy."

In other words, do you take too much to heart the opinion of people whose opinions don't really matter? If you are rejected by someone who doesn't really know you, then you are not being rejected for who you are. You are only being rejected for who that person *thinks* you are.

Rejection hurts. No doubt about it. But here are three very important things to remember about rejection:

1. It is entirely subjective. A person's reasons for turning you down are about them, not you.
2. Nothing ventured, nothing gained.
3. It won't kill you.

Rejection will never be easy, but it can get easier with practice. Ask anyone in sales and they'll tell you that learning to take no for an answer without crumbling into despair and self-loathing is key to success. Part of the trick is figuring out what soothes you when it happens. Time with a close friend who will tell you how swell you are? Immersing yourself in something you love to do and are good at? Hanging out with family that thinks you're the best thing since pay-at-the-pump?

Problems of insecurity and lack of self-confidence are beyond the scope of this book; there are many other books and professionals that can help with that. But introversion only gets in our way if we let it, and sometimes we can convince ourselves that we are being introverted when what we are really being is afraid.

Time for Love, or Maybe Not

Making Space in Your Life for One More Person

An introverted fellow in his twenties who is interested in finding love wrote to me asking how to find the energy to get to know a potential partner when all his energy goes into maintaining his friendships.

"I feel like someone would have to be a really good friend, before anything 'relationshippy' could even begin to grow," he wrote. "But here's the dilemma: Once I have a few really good friends, my energy resources are tapped out. So it feels like I'd have to 'dump' one of my friends to make room for someone new. This absolutely sucks, because . . . well . . . I like my friends!"

How do you make room for love when it's all you can do to make room for friends? Do you have to give up one to gain the other? I posed this question to my panel of introverts and got responses ranging from "I worry about that, too!" to "I have no idea what she's talking about."

"I think we can always find the time to do the things that we really enjoy and love; it's just a matter of managing our priorities," says Alan, a 46-year-old business analyst.

"I don't have a limited pool of energy that can be exhausted when it comes to maintaining friendships," Ray-Mel says. "I may not want to be around anybody, friend, stranger, or even myself, at times, but that's never a permanent or particularly long-term situation; that's just a recharging."

John, however, could relate to the predicament. "It's enough work for me to maintain my existing friendships, let alone find the time and energy to initiate a friendship/relationship—as all relationships must contain friendship. . . . At the end of my workday— which is quite people intensive, and which I am good at—I have very little energy to devote to fostering friendships or relationships."

Actually, this fellow who worried about keeping friends while finding a lover is not far off the mark. A 2014 study out of the University of Oxford found that we all seem to maintain a constant number of intimates, and when we add one, we drop one. While the number of people—what researchers call an individual's "social signature"—varies from person to person, each individual's social signature remains pretty constant.

So that's the bad news. Adding a one-and-only to your life could mean dropping someone else.

But let's face it: Despite a widespread sentimental belief that friendships are forever, in reality, friends come and go. Oh, they might stick around forever, in that Christmas cards and Facebook birthday greetings way. And we might maintain friends from way,

way back with whom we share an intimacy so deep that even if we see each other only occasionally, we can pick up where we left off. But close, day-to-day friendships tend to shift over time, depending on such things as proximity (a big player in friendship, though we hate to admit it) and stage of life (parents hang with parents, especially when children are young). If you hang with a bunch of single people, many of them will start drifting away when they couple up. Like it or not, that's the way it is.

So, there you go. You might have to drop a friend to have a lover. And if your energy is extremely limited, you might have to drop a friend to even find a lover, since dating and getting to know someone is energy intensive. Deciding how to parcel out your energy to friends versus potential mates is something only you can do for yourself.

If your close friends really are close friends, however, they will support you—even help you—in your search for love. They'll fix you up. They won't resent the time you spend dating. They'll stay your friends even if you're not available all the time. They'll be nice to the people you're dating. (And/or have your back if they suspect the person is any kind of no-goodnik.) With a bit of luck, your friends and your dates will actually like each other and you can all hang out together sometimes.

And your friends would surely join you in low-key introverted evenings, such as coming to your house to hang out and watch a movie. That way, you can recharge and visit at the same time. If your friends only want to hang out with you in groups, at bars, or when you've got your extroverted dog-and-pony show going, then maybe they don't truly appreciate the introvert you are. Are they the right friends for you?

Finally, there's the good news to look forward to down the road.

"I found comfort in being able to focus on a friend I'd have around a lot: my wife," says Tyler, who has been married for four and a half years. "I think as time has gone on, the energy drain from my marriage has gotten less as it has become more and more 'normal.' Subsequently, energy for other relationships has increased."

So, yeah, you might have to sacrifice some friend time in pursuit of love. But the payoff is that eventually you can have both, if you want.

One Isn't Necessarily the
Loneliest Number

Some People Are Meant to Be Single

Drew is an eligible young attorney who has dates, friends, and social life aplenty. But, he says, "I really, really don't see myself living with anyone. I just really enjoy the quiet of being alone. It's not like Monday through Friday I come home from work and never see anybody. But seeing somebody every night—just having somebody in the house, even if you're not talking to them, even if you're doing different things, there's still that pinging going on. . . ."

Sure, you might be thinking, he'll change his mind when the right someone comes along. Or you might be tempted to dismiss him as cold and selfish. Or you might wonder if there's something wrong with him.

But there's nothing at all wrong with Drew, and there are lots of other people who are just like him.

In fact, five million people in the United States between ages eighteen and thirty-four live alone, according to Eric Klinenberg, a sociologist and author of the book *Going Solo: The Extraordinary Rise and Surprising Appeal of Living Alone*. Most of the people living alone are between the ages of thirty-five and sixty-five and do it by choice.

And, by the way, some of those people who are living alone are not strictly single. After being married once and living with a woman for ten years, 51-year-old Eric, who trains people on heavy equipment (which requires a lot of interaction all day), swore off cohabiting. "I've come to the conclusion that I'm the kind of person who needs so much alone time that having a spouse in the house just doesn't work for me," he says. For the past five years, he's been in a committed relationship with a woman—also introverted—who, like him, owns and lives in her own home and, like him, is satisfied with the arrangement. They live about twenty miles apart and see each other weekly. "I go to her house and do all the honey-dos; when I travel out of town, she takes care of my dog," Eric says. "We have Saturday night date night, and then Sunday we take our dogs for an outing. We're both very much dog people."

Though Eric and his girlfriend are not married, their lifestyle resembles that of a small but growing number of people who are "living apart together" or maintaining "dual dwellings," says social psychologist Bella DePaulo, who is writing a book on the different ways Americans today live. "Probably six or seven percent of American adults are living apart together." Some are doing it because of various constraints—such as career commitments—but others do it by choice.

"Some of the people I've interviewed started out doing the traditional thing, then they realize, 'Oh my gosh, this is really not for me.' They still love the other person, they just don't love living with the other person," says DePaulo. "They move apart into their separate spaces, not as a step toward divorcing but toward saving the relationship."

But even beyond living arrangements, some people are simply meant to remain single says DePaulo, who also wrote *Singled Out: How Singles Are Stereotyped, Stigmatized, and Ignored, and Still Manage to Live Happily Ever After*. Some people are "single at heart," she says, and live happier, more fulfilling lives if they stay single than they would if they bought into society's mandate to couple up. And if you think you might be among them, DePaulo has reassuring news for you: That whole idea that singles are lonely and isolated is a myth.

"The evidence is really built up now that what's really isolating isn't singlehood, it's getting married," DePaulo says, pointing out that married people have less contact with friends, siblings, and other relatives. And she says, "There are American longitudinal studies that show that once they go from being single to being married, they're basically cutting people out of their lives and marginalizing them."

As a girl, DePaulo never fantasized about getting married. "I always thought, 'I'm just not bitten by the marriage bug yet,'" she says. But she eventually realized that she probably never would be. "Marriage is not who I am. I'm single and I actually want to be and that's not going to change."

It's kind of a revolutionary concept and perhaps hard to swallow. But sit with it a bit and see if it starts feeling less shocking.

The best way to know if you're single at heart, DePaulo says, is to examine your motives for wanting to stay single. Are they positive, or are you afraid, angry, or otherwise avoidant?

"It's an approach, it's not an avoidance," says DePaulo. "It's an approach to loving your solitude, loving your time alone, loving your self-sufficiency, liking to pursue the kinds of things that are most meaningful to you. There are all sorts of things that might make your own life meaningful that you might be able to pursue more. That's what I listen for; not the running away from relationships but the grasping and embracing what makes your life feel authentic."

So if you really do worry about fitting a full-time partner into your life, have you ever considered the possibility that you could live a fulfilling life without one? It's a radical thought and outside the norm, and just as introverts have felt a lot of pressure in our society to become more extroverted, single people feel a lot of pressure to become less single. But there is room for all kinds in our world. Are you, deep down, looking for permission to stay single? Well, then, permission granted. You can make time for whatever is most important to you, and no law says it has to be love and marriage.

PART II

Where Is Love? And How?

Meeting, Dating, Connecting

Just Say Yes

Because You Won't Find Love in Your Living Room

A while back, I ran a survey on my blog asking introverts how they meet people. More than 44 percent of those who responded checked "Beats me, I have trouble meeting people."

"Meeting new people is hard enough; meeting new potential romantic partners is even harder," says Joy, a 35-year-old library sciences student.

True. And there are a lot of reasons for that.

For one thing, introverts aren't likely to strike up conversations just for the hell of it because we're so averse to banal conversation.

"There's something inherently annoying to me about talking to most people," says Taylor. "It's painfully obvious when they aren't really listening and responding, but just waiting for you to stop talking. There's a reason I don't talk much; it usually feels like a waste."

In addition, because we're not always good at deactivating our

excellent listening skills, even when we're bored, if we do get en-
snared by a windbag or chatterbox, we have trouble extricating
ourselves. I have seen the sands of time slipping away, the end of
my life coming ever closer, while sitting glazed-eyed through a
once-casual conversation that has morphed into an interminable
monologue. So I'm pretty cautious about when and where I let
myself be pulled into chitchat.

Introverts also tend to turn down invitations we're not gung-ho
about, which may cause us to limit our socializing to the same
people. We like who we like and we like hanging around with
people we like a lot more than we like hanging around with people
we don't know. So if no one among our intimates is a likely candi-
date for love, or if we've cycled through all possible prospects and
still ended up single, then our default social life isn't much help
when it comes to finding romance.

And even if we do venture out into larger society, it can take us
a while to warm up to new people. Meeting someone interesting
at a party may or may not go anywhere if our time with them is
limited.

Still, one of the best things you can do while you're looking for
love is accept any invitations that don't sound unbearable. Just say
yes. Say yes when you're invited to a friend's birthday celebration
dinner. Say yes to that fund-raiser for a favorite cause (bring an
extroverted friend if you need support). Say yes when that favorite
author comes to town for a reading and signing; waiting in line to
get a book signed provides ample opportunity for easy conversation

with people around you. Say yes to anything that brings you in contact with people with whom you have something in common.

More than one of the introverts I spoke to met their partners when they said yes to an invitation to happy hour. Gary, a 61-year-old pastor, said yes when a friend invited him to celebrate a tax refund with a friend of his. "I was attracted to my present wife from the moment I saw her standing with our mutual friend and another woman at my door," he remembers. And his wife, I might add, is also an introvert who also obviously said yes. So just say yes and show up. Commit to staying an hour. If it doesn't work out for you, just leave. No harm, no foul.

OK, you're allowed to say no if you think the event might provoke introvert catatonia. I shut down in really large parties where I know few people. I may or may not perform well at professional networking events, depending on how large they are and whether I have something in common with others. Events with people who are all in my field are much easier to deal with than more general networking events where I have to search for common ground with people I meet. (Ugh, I shudder to think about how tongue-tied I got at a general networking event I recently attended in a moment of just-say-yes fervor. Mistake.)

As well as introducing you to new people at their parties or other get-togethers, friends who know you well can be an excellent source of blind dates—something else to say yes to.

"The best first date I ever went on was a blind date where I didn't know anything at all about the girl," Drew says. "My friend Laura said, 'Hey, I have a friend you should date,' and made reservations for us at a restaurant. We got along fantastically well and dated for about half a year." (Props to Laura for actually making reservations for Drew and her friend, thereby making it just a matter of showing up for both of them. Smooth move.)

In general, Drew is down with the blind date. "I enjoy meeting someone and having no idea what they're like, what their interests are, or even if we'll get along with each other," he says. "It's like seeing a movie when I've never seen the trailer. I may love it, or I may hate it, but either way, it's only an hour and a half, and if it's dreadfully bad, I can always leave." (And he has, though he did make it through the meal and pay the check before fleeing.)

Blind dates might sound scary, but really—what can it hurt? You go out, you meet a new person, you either have a good time or a not-so-good time, you either feel chemistry or you don't, and then you go on with your life, with or without this person. If it doesn't work out, it only cost you a few hours of your time. (And any money you may have spent on the date.) But sometimes it does work out.

There used to be an ad for a state lottery that cautioned, "You can't win it if you're not in it." That's pretty good all-purpose advice, and it especially applies here. If your life entails going round and round in the same circles, you limit your chances of meeting someone wonderful. So when unusual opportunities arise, say yes, show up, and see what happens. You just never know.

Smile from the Inside Out

The Art of Appearing Approachable

As the old saw goes, 80 percent of life is showing up, and in the following chapters we're going to talk about ways and places you can show up to increase your opportunities to meet someone special.

Of course, as we discussed, even if you spend your life among fabulous, fascinating people, if your protective introvert force field is activated at all times, you're keeping yourself perpetually on the outside looking in. You need to go into these situations prepared to be approachable.

I understand most of us don't want to look approachable all the time. Sometimes all you really want is to be left alone, and that's fine. For those moments, we know how to put out a "leave me alone" vibe. Turn away from the room. Bury ourselves in a book or our phone. Avoid eye contact. Close off our posture, with crossed arms and legs. It all works, except for those most determined to make contact with you, which can be either a good thing (this is a nice person who finds something about you irresistible) or bad (this is an annoying person with no sense of personal boundaries).

Being able to evoke boundaries is a good skill for an introvert. But it can backfire if you haven't developed the ability to turn off that body language when you want to. Even when you're not saying a word, your body language speaks volumes. And there are a lot of situations where you want your body to send the message that you're confident and open to meeting people. So while it might feel awkward at first, being able to turn on approachability at will is a useful skill to develop.

I believe that the first step to looking approachable is thinking approachable. It's no big news that our minds and bodies work in collaboration, one feeding off the other. Radio announcers and telemarketers know, for example, that keeping a smile on their face puts a smile in their voice. Similarly, going into a situation with "approachable" on your mind can help your body exude approachability.

Amy Cuddy, a social scientist who studies the role nonverbal communication plays in personal power, has learned that you can "fake it till you make it" with nonverbal communication. No matter how you feel in any situation, if you take a confident or powerful stance, taking up space rather than folding into yourself, you are likely not only to look more confident/powerful, but you'll feel that way, too.

In fact, Cuddy's research found that taking a power pose (for example, hands on your hips like Wonder Woman) increases testosterone (the power hormone) and decreases cortisol (the stress hormone). So she suggests that before you go into any stressful situation where you feel like you'll be judged (hello, party/networking event/first day of classes), find a private place (hello, bathroom) and stand with your arms up and extended, feet apart—she describes it as a starfish—for two minutes. It sounds crazy, but it will actually cause physiological changes in your body that will help you go into the situation feeling more confident and powerful.

Once you feel confident or ready to try, then you'll want to do the opposite of all those leave-me-be things listed above. Face the room. Put away the book and phone. Uncross whatever is crossed. Think about relaxing your muscles so you don't look stiff. (I like leaning if I possibly can—on a wall, on a bar, on a high table. For whatever reason, that makes me feel much more at ease.) Try to control nervous habits, like knee bouncing or cuticle picking. Look around you openly, with genuine interest. If you make eye contact with someone, let a little smile flit across your lips. It doesn't have to be an overbearing "let's be friends" grin. Just a little twitch of the lips, a friendly acknowledgment.

Be aware, though, that a smile of the mouth only, one that doesn't involve the eyes, is not perceived as genuine. Cuddy recommends that you actually think of something that makes you smile—even if it's just how ridiculous you feel trying to smile at a stranger.

If someone does start a conversation with you, be receptive, regardless of whether or not you think there's any love connection potential there. First of all, that conversation will confirm to you that your approachable vibe is coming across. Second, you want other people to see that you are, indeed, approachable. Third, it's only polite.

Introverts mostly don't need coaching in listening; we tend to be very good listeners. But for some of us, eye contact in conversation can be difficult. How much is too much? How much is too little? Eye contact is definitely a nonverbal signal of interest and confidence, and it makes people respond positively to you. If you're not naturally comfortable with it, focus on developing it more. In an article titled "4 Reasons Why You Don't Get Noticed at Networking Events (and She Does)," career expert Kara Ronin suggests you practice by looking into the other person's eyes while you're listening, which can be easier than eye contact while you're talking.

When you're ready to end a conversation, try letting your eyes wander from the speaker. That should send the message.

In many ways, nonverbal communication is more powerful than the verbal kind, which can be good news for those of us who don't chatter. But to make nonverbal communication work for us, we have to know how to work it.

People, People Everywhere

Opportunities to Connect in Everyday Life

Unless you're a hard-core recluse (in which case, the chapter on dating in cyberspace is for you), chances are pretty good that the ordinary life you live affords plenty of opportunities for finding someone to love. Taking advantage of everyday opportunities just requires stepping out from inside your head so that possibilities don't just slip past while you're busy ruminating. Being lucky in love might be less a matter of luck and more a matter of paying attention.

Meeting people is not a discrete event that happens only when you have set out to meet people. Tens, dozens, even hundreds of people pass through our lives every day (depending on what sort of life you lead). Opportunities to connect can be everywhere if you keep yourself open to possibilities. This is not always easy for introverts who haven't learned how to let down their leave-me-alone force field, but, as we've discussed, an ability to be open to opportunity is a skill worth developing. And note I say "an ability." In other words, you don't have to let down that force field permanently. Again, you just want to be in control of it, to notice when you're in the mood and/or in a situation when it would benefit you to open yourself up to possibilities.

College is essentially the last time and place in life when you are thrown together with a huge number and variety of peers, so it's not surprising that many people meet their spouse in college. While the idea of college as a happy hunting ground for mates is kind of retro (especially when you're talking about women), it's hard to completely rule out the notion. Lots of people, lots of parties, lots of potential. And the intensity of grad school is its own sort of aphrodisiac.

Once you're out of school, however, meeting people gets a little trickier. You'll meet people on the job, of course. While many will be age-inappropriate or already in a relationship, and of course we all know to exercise extreme caution when it comes to on-the-job romance (especially for the awkwardness that would follow a breakup), it certainly can't hurt to keep your eyes open at work.

Many of the introverts I spoke to who are in relationships met their partners in an organic fashion—through friends, at church, and (cautiously) at work.

"We worked together for a while and got to know each other day to day," says 42-year-old Beth, who is not only an introvert married to an introvert, but is also a professional coach focused on introverted entrepreneurs. "There wasn't anything quick about it; it evolved in the ordinary," she says. She was dating someone else when they met, but she and her now-husband often walked home together after work. "The walks home gave us a chance to talk about sensitive topics," she recalls. "When you think about it, so many important conversations happen when you aren't expected to make regular eye contact with the other person."

Then he gave her a mix tape, "a secret message," she says. "It did some of the heavy communication lifting for him." (Ah yes, the mix tape. The mating call of the introvert. I've made, and received, many.) They've been married for sixteen years now.

So yes, you do want to be careful about on-the-job romance (and your HR department can tell you any company rules on that subject), but that doesn't mean you can't keep it in the back of your mind. Maybe it's not someone in your company but someone interesting who rides the elevator with you each morning. Or someone in a department remote enough from yours (for example, you're art department, she's accounting) that if things go south, you won't have to work together every day. Maybe you'll get a new job and before you leave, you can wink at the coworker who's been on your mind all along.

Having regular haunts, where everybody knows your name, also opens up opportunities. Anne, a 50-year-old stay-at-home mom, said yes when the owner of a local Christian bookstore she frequented offered to set her up with another customer, also an introvert. "She talked to him about me and me about him. He was male and he was a Christian, so I was the one she thought of."

Married twenty-one years now.

Is there a shop you visit regularly? Can't hurt to get on friendly terms with the proprietor, who sees a lot of people every day. (One good reason among many, by the way, to patronize small, independent stores over big-box stores.)

When he worked at night, Eric would often stop for "exactly two drinks" at a low-key bar where there were rarely any other patrons in his age bracket (most were younger). So one night when he saw an age-appropriate woman there, he struck up a conversation. "I am good at small talk when I'm motivated," he says. They've been dating five years now.

Do you get your coffee at the same place at the same time every day? Chances are other people do, too. Do you just dash in and out or do you hang out? (More on meeting people in such public places later.)

How about meals? A lot of people find dining alone awkward, but doing it at a restaurant bar can be easier and often quite convivial. Make yourself a regular and you're bound to meet others—and not all barflies if it's also a restaurant. Many will be other people who just don't feel like cooking.

And your close social circle is, of course, the heart of your network; you never know who will turn up among the people you see regularly. My husband and I ran in the same circles—in fact, long before we met at a mutual friend's barbecue, I attended a large and raucous party at his house without ever encountering him (it was that kind of party). After we met, I started running into him in all sorts of places my circle habituated. At an art gallery opening. A bowling party. Another gallery opening. And finally at a party where I noticed he was being pursued by another woman and decided I'd better make myself perfectly clear or risk missing out. I was quite forward, asking if he wanted my telephone number and smooching him in the parking lot. He called me soon after, we went to the movies, yada yada yada, married more than twenty-five years now.

The bottom line in all this is that the world is full of people and life can be full of opportunities, but only if you approach them all with an open mind and adventurous spirit. And at the same time, it also can't hurt to place yourself in situations that increase your chances of making a connection, whether it's finding a coffee shop to make your own, or showing up wherever your type of people show up. Or both. The more the merrier.

Parties

Like It or Not,
They Are Rife with Possibilities

Parties. Sigh. People tell us they're fun, but are they? Really?

Well . . . um . . . sometimes. To some of us. Under certain circumstances.

I have heard from introverts who say they wouldn't dream of attending a party, and I understand that. But for me there's a certain sweet spot of parties—not too big, not too small, mostly people I know. I have genuine fun at those parties. It's big parties that I find stressful, especially if I tell myself that unless I have circulated and schmoozed and met a bunch of new people, then I have failed at party guesting.

The thing is, though, parties really are a good way to put yourself in proximity to a bunch of people who are mostly vetted by the party's host. (Provided we're not talking about a massive frat party free-for-all or some such.) If you know and like your host, chances are pretty good there will be at least a handful of other people at the party you also will like.

One key to party survival—even pleasure—is to approach them with the mind-set that you will do them your way. In other words, rather than feeling like a failure because you can't work a party like an extrovert, try approaching parties feeling comfortable with your introversion and introverted ways. That way, you won't feel like a poor excuse for an extrovert; you'll feel like a fabulous example of an introvert. After all, the way I see it, the only obligation you have as a party guest is to enjoy yourself. If sitting in a corner and watching is your idea of fun, then fie on anyone who tries to tell you otherwise. You are entitled to party any way you like.

So, let's say yes to the next party invitation and see who's there.

Think you might want to meet an extrovert? It's pretty easy to tell who those are. They come boogalooing into the room. Their smiles scan the crowd like the beam of a lighthouse. They're all over the place, introducing themselves to strangers and introducing friends to each other, regaling people with stories and jokes, getting the action going on the dance floor. Their eyes are always on the move, keeping track of who's doing what where at the party, looking for their next conversation/dance/new friend.

Introverts, on the other hand, are hiding in plain sight, lingering on the edges of the party. They might be hanging by the food table, where minglers come to them. They might be standing silently in conversational circles. They might be keeping busy with little chores in the kitchen; if your hosts don't set you up with a drink the minute you arrive, chances are pretty good that the person who does is an introvert. You'll see introverts examining the host's bookshelves or artwork. They're talking to the dog. They're hiding in the bathroom. (Don't go looking for them there; it's rude. But if you see someone heading for the bathroom more than once during a party, that person is either a big beer drinker or an introvert.)

They might be sitting in comfortable places watching the scene around them, or in quiet conversation with another introvert. You know that image where you look at it one way and it's Freud's face and you look at it differently and it's a naked lady? And you know how once you see the naked lady, you can't unsee it? Introverts are like that. No, not naked (yet). But once you adjust your eyes to look for introverts, you'll see them all over.

So, after you've spotted someone who seems interesting . . . then what?

With extroverts, no big whoop. You know they want to meet people, so just make your way toward the one who interests you and see what happens.

Meeting another introvert can require more finesse, especially for those of us sensitive to the needs of other introverts and reluctant to intrude on their quiet space. "Do I go to a party and just look out for someone else in a quiet corner and be like, 'Wanna go read *The Neverending Story* outside?'" an introvert asked in a blog comment. "You can't approach someone while they're doing their quiet-time thing, because let's be honest: I wouldn't want to be bothered, either, when I'm chilling on a couch, timing out to some music."

Nope, I disagree completely. I think you can safely assume that, just by dint of their presence at the party, everybody there is open to conversation. Even the introvert on the couch is fair game. I would argue that even introverts are silently and perhaps even fervently hoping for conversation, though they're not likely to be working the room. I liken myself to a sea sponge at parties, sitting in one place and digesting any conversation that drifts by me. While you might be taking a risk if you approach someone, I promise you that you're not breaking any unspoken rule by talking to anyone who catches your interest at a party.

Try to let go of the fear of being too forward. Introverts' bar for being pushy is set so low that even saying hi can feel like we're being intrusive. Be assured that the pushiest introvert at the party probably isn't as aggressive as the lowest-key extrovert there. Get as pushy as you can stand, and at the very worst you'll probably just come across as friendly. That's a good thing.

And crank down your sensitive introvert radar a few notches, too. Many introverts are extremely tuned in to the unspoken messages of people around us—which is helpful at times, but obstructive at other times. Our radars aren't foolproof and they might pick up ambivalence or anxiety and assume it's rejection. Maybe it is, maybe it isn't. If it clearly is, shrug and move on. Remember that it can't be personal if the person doesn't know you, so don't let it throw you off your game. You never know if you don't try.

You'll also want to come up with a plan for when you want to extricate yourself from a conversation; parties are one of those places where introverts' good listening skills can be a liability if you're not exactly enjoying the conversation. Fleeing to the bathroom, of course, is tried and true. Or excuse yourself to refresh your drink— even if the person decides to come with you, the movement and encounters with other people should send the conversation off the rails, freeing you to move on. Calling a friend over can help loosen one-on-one conversational ties. (Did you come to the party with a friend? Maybe you can prearrange a "rescue me" signal.) Or you could simply say, "Well, I think it's time for me to do some min- gling," and wander off. That's what you're expected to do at parties anyway.

I understand that parties are not on the top of many introverts' fun list. But if you're looking for love, then they're fertile ground. If you can't think of them as fun, think of them as productive. If you don't actually look forward to them, at least approach them with an open mind. Go for as long as you can, bring an extroverted friend if that helps (although you might find yourself on your own anyway, as your friend spins off into extrovert fun), and don't put a lot of pressure on yourself. Just give it a shot.

And if you can't seem to make a connection at the party, that doesn't mean you're doing it wrong or you're a loser or deficient in some way. Sometimes a good time is had by all, sometimes not so much. If you've given the party a good try and it's just going flat on you, pat yourself on the back for showing up to begin with, and leave without angst, guilt, or shame. Because the best way to get yourself to go to parties in the first place is to let yourself go home when you've had enough.

The More the Maybe-er

The Potential in Group Activities

It's age-old advice for people who need people: Join a group.

Yeah, I'm not much of a joiner, either. I couldn't tell you why, exactly, except that there are few things I enjoy that require the participation of others. Still, if you want to meet a lot of people who have interests similar to yours, joining a group is kind of a no-brainer.

Keep in mind, though, that the only way to make group events work for you is if you go into them with the mind-set that you are going to remain open to interaction (refer back to the chapter on approachability). In general, don't be afraid to look around; smile at people if you can; don't bury yourself in a book or your phone any time you're not otherwise engaged; don't sit in the farthest corner of the classroom and bolt the moment class is over.

As much as possible, exercise whatever chitchat skills you have—you might find that chitchat isn't as odious as usual if you've chosen an activity that truly interests you, since you can focus on whatever common interest brought you together with these people in the first place. And talk to anyone who seems interesting, or who strikes up a conversation with you, whether or not the person is a potential romantic partner. Others might be drawn into your conversation, and any conversation puts out the signal that you are open to meeting people.

Formal groups around a specific interest have all kinds of benefits. To begin with, there's the shared-interest benefit: Here is a group of people with whom you'll have at least one thing in common. Additionally, group meetings are likely to have an agenda, so you won't have to freestyle mingle the entire time. You will have time to chat either before or after the program; unless you've attended a meeting already and have made some connections, post-agenda mingling might be easier, since the presentation should have provided fodder for discussion.

If you're shy, persuade a friend to join you the first time you attend the meeting. Even an introverted friend can be helpful, since conversation between the two of you can, if you're not huddled together in a corner, be an implicit invitation for others to join in.

Your own life, interests, and experiences provide all sorts of clues to kinds of groups that might suit you.

Go with the pros: A professional organization in your field is a great way to meet kindred spirits. Brett, a 30-year-old public relations professional, met his soul mate at a young professionals organization. "We were both heavy into the community service aspect and we bonded over that," he says. Professional organizations also have meetings or get-togethers with specific agendas or tasks. Best of all, professional organizations often have online discussion boards, where you can get to know people in the virtual world before you meet them face to face, kind of like online dating, but less stressful. I've made good friends through writers' forums, and seen love bloom among members of a professional organization I belonged to; it germinated online, took root at conferences, and ultimately blossomed into marriage. Pretty cool.

Revisit your past: I've also seen love connections made through an online forum for my high school graduating class; the two people knew each other but were not romantically involved in our teen years. Yeah, I know high school was tough for a lot of people—and perhaps especially introverts—and maybe you can't imagine why you would want to reconnect with people from back then. But I suggest you reconsider. A shared background can be very powerful, and depending on how long ago you graduated, you might find people greatly changed. If your graduating class has a Facebook page, hang out there awhile. It's low commitment and you can see what others are up to. You just never know who might turn out to be a lot more compelling and less annoying than they were when you were sixteen.

Name your pleasure: Another option is seeking out a group focused on an activity you enjoy, where meeting people is a secondary benefit rather than the focal point of the activity. Join a community orchestra. A gardening club. Take a painting class. Or a class in accounting for small businesses. Or some sort of esoteric literature class. Whatever turns you on. It's much easier to talk to strangers when you are all truly engaged in what you're doing than it is if the whole activity centers around talking to strangers. (Networking events = Just shoot me.) Introvert Melissa met one of her boyfriends at Amtgard, "a medieval combat recreation social club." Speaking of esoteric interests.

Book clubs are theoretically a good idea for introverts, but if you're a woman looking to meet men, you might be disappointed because book clubs tend to attract women and couples. If you're a man looking to meet women, then by all means, find yourself a book club. Bookstores often sponsor clubs or provide meeting spaces.

Get online: Meetup.com is another frequently recommended way to meet people in groups; you can look for gatherings focused on specific interests or singles groups in your area, as Robert did after his divorce. "I did end up dating several women over the course of a few years, got kind of involved with some of them, and ended up with a group of really good friends, if not a relationship." He still attends group activities sometimes. "Turns out I like playing trivia," he says.

Work it out: Even fitness classes can be good if they are at a time, such as weekends, when people might be likely to dillydally before and after. Shared moaning and groaning about the challenges of the workout, sore muscles, and what you think about the instructor are good springboards for further conversation. Boot camp classes are more likely to be a balance of men and women than, say, yoga, although there are usually a few men sprinkled among the women at larger yoga classes. Team sports can allow easy entrée to conversation if you so desire; if not, you can just concentrate on the game. If you're really good at it, people will be coming to meet you anyway.

Go natural: Outdoor activities are attractive to all kinds of people. Bird-watchers are a passionate bunch that often flock together; runners and cyclists also like to form groups. Elizabeth belongs to a hiking club, which is nice because her girlfriend isn't much of a hiker. Adventure travel tours, especially the kind that require an expert guide (white-water rafting, for example, or long-distance bike tours), attract a variety of people, and the experience itself facilitates bonding. In fact, research finds a correlation between adrenaline and attraction—a shot of the former tends to boost the latter. So if you've ever dreamed of rafting the Grand Canyon, you can wait years to get a permit to do it yourself (if you have the skills), or you can do it with a reputable outfitter and meet other adventurous sorts on a group trip. And the thrill of the ride might up the amps of any love connection you make.

Hit the road: Travel in general provides all kinds of opportunities to join groups of interesting people. Granted, tour-group travel can be rough on introverts; you want to be sure you're capable of resisting peer pressure to always run with the crowd in order to eke out necessary time for yourself. (Though it's more costly, having a hotel room to yourself helps a lot. When I travel with a group, I often set my alarm for an hour or two before we are scheduled to meet in order to have time to myself. Sometimes I'll splurge on room service breakfast rather than eating with the gang.)

Even if you don't join a group, however, if you travel with an extroverted friend, you will probably meet people. Sometimes that can be annoying, sometimes it can be wonderful.

You also might find it surprisingly easy to meet people when traveling completely alone. If not focused on a traveling companion, you might find yourself feeling more open to meeting people. Joining a walking tour of a city, for example, or a docent tour of a museum are casual, comfortable ways to chat with strangers, and they last just an hour or two. If nothing else, you'll learn some cool stuff.

Afiq, a 24-year-old medical student who is single, experienced this solo-travel phenomenon for the first time not long ago, while visiting a cousin in Egypt. He was staying in a hotel and spent some time hanging around the lobby with his laptop. "All of a sudden, I had this urge to initiate conversation, or at least when someone said hi to me, I tried to make conversation," he says. "Maybe it's a good thing I was on my own! Even though I'm an introvert, that doesn't mean I can't talk to others, right?" Right, Afiq! And right on, right on!

Love in Your Living Room

Dating in Cyberspace

OK, I lied before when I said the love of your life wasn't going to just show up in your living room. There is one way that might happen.

"The Internet is the introvert dater's best friend," says Doug M., who met his new (introverted) wife online.

Drew also likes dabbling in online dating. "It's a little dopamine rush when you check your email."

Which sounds pretty fun.

Although I met my husband long before the miracle of the Internet, I see the appeal of online dating. And I've had quite a few friendships develop online: We met online, got to know each other online, and by the time we finally met in person, we were already friends. It was like online dating, but platonic.

Before he met his wife, Doug tried a few dating websites and connected with quite a few women. Sometimes he could tell after a couple of messages that there was no potential love connection (and being a gentleman, he would let them know they didn't seem like a good fit). All in all, he went out on "a fair number" of dates over the course of a couple of years. Online introductions made first dates easier, he says. "The small talk of first dates is basically my version of hell," he says. "With online dating, you have that initial interaction through writing and can take the time to collect your thoughts and edit things. It's a little less daunting."

Although some people take to online dating easily, others are skeptical. Chris says, "I lump the promises of online love right along with the promises of a fortune coming from a deposed African prince. There is so much anonymity behind a computer, and while that's a great tool for me when I want to limit my interactions with people, it seems counterintuitive toward starting an intimate relationship." Mike, 43, who does sales support for a tech company, says that while he enjoys the online part of online dating, it doesn't make talking on the phone or meeting any less intimidating.

Taylor has tried it, but has serious reservations. "I don't like how pathetic it makes me feel, stalking around looking at girls' photos and trying to think of something absolutely fascinating to message her and get her attention."

I get that, but suggest it can be reframed: Going online to try to find a partner is proactive and shows determination, not desperation.

And while I'm pretty sure the experience is different for women and men (for one thing, women are much more likely to receive horrifically inappropriate messages—Melissa swore it off for that reason), the way Rebecca approached online dating sounds anything but desperate. She was discerning, and went into the venture with high standards.

"Since personal communication started out as emails rather than in person, I was able to gauge even more before deciding to meet them," she says. "At the top of my list of wants, I was looking for intelligence and humor. I was interpreting and making judgments about them from their writing. Could they string coherent sentences together with correctly spelled words? What was the level of their vocabulary? Were they witty? Did they pay attention to the things I wrote?

"Putting this into words makes it sound like I was cold and calculating, and maybe I was," she says. "I was methodical, and perhaps the key for me was that I was in control and protected during this process. Meeting in person was the final step rather than the first step."

Before they met, Doug and his now-wife took their online getting-to-know-you phase even further. After Doug made the first move, sending the initial email, he endured a very long forty-eight-hour wait until she responded. ("I was crushed that she wasn't sitting by the computer waiting for my email," he says.) At the beginning of their correspondence, she Googled him (who among us hasn't?) and found his blog. "She owned up to it immediately," Doug says, and since she also blogged, they swapped links and each of them did a little independent research. "It helped the conversation in real life, not having to drag out all these things in person."

Which brings me to another point: Meeting people online

doesn't always mean going to online dating sites. The explosion of online social networking means cyberspace is full of parties to join. You can banter on Twitter, look through others' eyes on Instagram, swap book recommendations on Goodreads.

This approach worked for 41-year-old Don, an author who also does IT support. "My current girlfriend and I are both authors so we ended up following each other on Twitter, then graduated to emails, then to phone calls, then to meeting in person," he says. "It's what I'm most comfortable with."

I've seen people strike up conversations in the comments of my introvert blog (although if any love connections were ever made, I don't know about it). I've seen friends hit it off in the comments of my posts on Facebook; a couple have even dated. In general, you can treat your online social network like a "real" social network and keep alert for possibilities there, too. Look for interesting people in the comments of friends' posts. If you're feeling bold, ask your friend for more information. I've had friends of friends friend me. (Did you follow that?) It's not out of line.

But back to dating sites. No, you don't have to want to do it. No judging. If you're intrigued but intimidated, however, if you've tried it but haven't felt successful, or if you just want to up your game, there are actually experts out there who can help—such as online dating coach Kimberly Dawn Neumann, who gave me some great tips.

First of all, she points out that free sites are more likely to attract people who are just playing around with the idea—or playing around in general. If you're commitment-minded, commit to a pay site.

In your profile, focus on what makes you, you. "You're looking to attract someone who is intrigued by the real you, not someone you *think* a person would like to date," Kimberly says. "Also, highlighting your unique traits can help provide entrée into online conversation. By the four hundredth profile they've read that claims liking candlelit dinners and walks on the beach, their eyes might be glazing over . . . until they happen upon your profile where you mention you have a penchant for making homemade bread or dabbling in archery or whatever." (Or you might include a photo of yourself hugging a horse, which is what drew Rebecca to the profile of the man she eventually married. If you don't have a horse, a ferret would probably be just as intriguing. Or a black lab. Or a Siamese cat. Or a hedgehog. Or a life-sized cutout of Albert Einstein. Whatever you've got.)

But don't try so hard to be interesting that you start making stuff up. Don't lie. It will only come back to bite you. OK, if you want to fudge your age a little to try to show up in a search bracket that you otherwise wouldn't, that's moderately permissible, Kimberly says, provided you 'fess up in one of the first emails. But lying about height or personal appearance? Bad idea. And no, they won't forget all about it once they get to know you; instead, you've started out by being a person they're not sure they can trust. "Remember, you're not looking to sell some version of yourself you cannot ever possibly live up to," Kimberly says. "You'll be found out anyway.

Your goal needs to be to present an accurate representation of yourself such that the right person who finds you appealing *just as you are* can locate you online!"

Also, no matter how sheepish you feel about looking for love online, keep that to yourself. Starting your profile with something glum like "I really don't know why I'm here" is a turnoff. Maybe you don't know why you're there, but everyone else does: You want to meet someone. That's nothing to be ashamed of. "There's enough insecurity in dating, so daters are more likely to respond to someone who seems fun and positive," says Kimberly.

And while it's OK to include what you're looking for in a mate, keep the wish list to a minimum. "Too many requirements can scare people away," Kimberly says. That said, you can include your deal breakers—if you absolutely, positively won't date a smoker, for example, go ahead and say so. Otherwise, stay positive and open-minded.

If you're like Rebecca and have a solid concept of the person you're looking for, look for clues in profiles. "People who write almost nothing in their profiles are probably not taking the whole thing very seriously," Kimberly says. (Alternately, Tone, who met her husband online, says that she found people who write scads and scads on their profiles tend to be self-centered and "take up a lot of space. I met a few of those and, needless to say, we did not click in any way.")

If all the photos a person posts are of themselves partying with a posse, that means this person probably spends a lot of time partying with a posse, which may or may not be what you're looking for.

And, of course, Kimberly adds, "anyone who gets too sexual too fast and posts lots of provocative photos is probably not looking online for someone to bring home to Mom!"

When is it time to take it off-line and into the real world? Go with your gut on that. But, Kimberly cautions, don't let the emailing drag on too long. She knows how we introverts are. "It might feel very comfy to just keep it online, where getting to know someone through words supplants the energy drain that comes from interacting vis-à-vis. The danger here is that you create this online relationship that starts to get too intimate before you've ever met in person. What happens if you do all this sharing and then the in-person chemistry isn't there when you are finally in front of each other? It makes it so much harder to politely move on to the next person if you've already had a full online relationship for weeks or months. There can be hurt feelings, disappointment, and way too much pressure on that first meeting if you wait too long to take it off-line."

And while this might not be a risk for the average picky introvert, Kimberly also cautions about getting caught up in "the supermarket syndrome"—filling your cart with every profile that seems mildly intriguing. "You can get easily overwhelmed," she says. "It's best to really think about what you're looking for and respond selectively, lest you burn out on online dating before you ever really get going." Like any other social interaction, online dating takes energy. "Set aside a certain amount of time per week to devote to searching for matches and responding to emails that interest you, but don't let it take over your life," Kimberly says.

And finally, Elizabeth, who met her girlfriend online, urges you to hang in there through disappointments. "Try not to get discouraged," she says. "I think we have a tendency to get our hopes up that the first person we meet will be 'the one.' It can be a real emotional letdown when that doesn't happen, and there's a good chance that it won't. You might have to meet a dozen or more people before you would even consider a second date with someone."

Do You Hide Here Often?

How to Hit On an Introvert

#introvertpickuplines from Twitter:

I'm not quite sure how to say this so I won't.

How 'bout I go back to my place?

I wish I were an extrovert so it would be easier to talk to you.

Come here and sit quietly in a corner often?

Hey, that's a great book, but you should keep reading it, and I'm really sorry I interrupted you.

You look as uncomfortable as I feel, and I mean that in a good way.

Hey, I noticed you noticing me, so I pretended to look at something on my phone.

A little awkwardness is cute, right? Good . . . I'm about to be painfully adorable.

As you might imagine, meeting other introverts requires some finesse. However daunting it may seem, though, you have the benefit of knowing what does and doesn't work for you, so you should have a general idea of what other introverts might be receptive to and what will make them run for the bathroom (introverts' favorite hiding place).

Naturally, you know better than trying to start a conversation with one of the irritating statements or observations that extroverts have subjected us to so many times. Things like, "Why are you so quiet?" or "Are you having fun?" If you're at a party, I also advise that you don't plunge right in with snide cracks about the extroverted goings-on, as one introvert suggested on my blog. Those extroverts you're cracking wise about might be that introvert's best friends.

And I'd avoid the risky strategy of drinking yourself to extroversion, although just to prove you should never say never, that did work for Julie, who met her introverted boyfriend at a party when they were freshmen in college. "My roommate at the time had been invited and I tagged along," she recalls. "We were playing drinking games and I just noticed him and thought he was really attractive. I asked around to see if he was single and he was, so I just wrote down my number and gave it to him.

"It was kind of out of personality for me, so I was a little embarrassed," she admits. But he texted her the very next morning, and now they are out of college and living together.

So, yeah, it can work. But better if you stop at happy tipsy and don't go to rip-roaring drunk, which is much more likely to lead to a middle-of-the-night shame attack than a date with a good-looking stranger.

For an opening line, straightforward never hurts, even with introverts—or maybe even especially with introverts. Opening gambits don't need to be clever or dazzling, just friendly. You can never go wrong at a party by just walking up to someone and saying hi and starting a conversation: "How do you know the host?" or "Do you know what this music is?"

But if that sounds intimidating, a more subtle technique if you spot an interesting introvert at a party is to try sitting or standing nearby, as if you just happen to be standing or sitting there for your own reasons, minding your own business. Try to be close enough to talk, but at a respectful distance. Make a random comment about the music, the food, or the décor. Maybe there's a coffee-table book you can pick up and flip through.

Slip into conversation casually. Be cool, be calm, don't stress, don't force it. If there's some silence, let it be. If your palms get sweaty, remind yourself that this is a situation where people expect to be engaged in conversation, unlike public places such as coffee shops and bookstores, where they may or may not be there to make friends.

Still, don't rule out those public places. Striking up conversations in those can be intimidating, but it's not impossible if you're feeling brave. Being a regular at a coffee shop or bar, like Eric was when he met his girlfriend, gives you a little edge, since a chat with the bartender, waitperson, or barista can easily draw in others nearby. But even if you're not a regular, places where people linger provide ample opportunity for making connections.

If you spot someone interesting, first assess his or her body language: Sitting facing out toward the room or turned away from it? Looking up and around or pointedly buried in a book or laptop? Headphones are a pretty obvious "no, thanks" sign. A cell phone can go either way: It might mean the person is absorbed in a text conversation, it might just be something to fiddle with out of boredom or feeling awkward. Give it a shot. You'll be able to tell soon enough if you're intruding, and if you are, back off and don't worry about it.

Eye contact is always a strong indicator, as long as you don't get stuck in an introvert standoff. Furtive glances at each other will only take you so far. And by "so far," I mean "nowhere." Eventually somebody will have to step out of the introvert comfort zone; it might as well be you. And this goes for anyplace you might make an unplanned connection. When the lady with thirty items in the express lane at the supermarket takes out her checkbook to pay, exchanging a quick eye-roll with the cutie in front of you in line can provide entrée for a smile and friendly word about the price of rutabagas.

Do keep in mind, though, that being approached by strangers is an entirely different experience for men and women. In comments on my blog, introverted guys begged women to have mercy and make the first move sometimes.

"As a guy, I'm always open to conversation from interesting

women," one wrote. "If you make eye contact, smile, and I smile back, that means 'Hello. Come over. Sit down. I really want to talk, but I'm shy and insecure.' Really, women hold the cards here. They're usually more selective than men regarding dating, and so guys like me (who are already insecure) are liable to not take the shot."

"As a strong introvert, and a single guy, being approached by a smart interesting woman *never* gets old," another wrote. "I think a simple 'hi' or something like 'nice jacket' or anything simple and sweet to break the ice is just fine. Something funny never gets old, either."

Women are less encouraging and more cautious. Blame some of your comrades in testosterone; live through enough catcalls, inappropriate comments, and lounge-lizard approaches and you tend to get a little jaded about men striking up conversation.

"The last couple of times I have had that happen, the opening comments from the person initiating have set off my 'creep alert' pretty fast," one woman wrote. "Usually this happens one of two ways—either attempting to touch me, or moving beside me instead of across from me where I can see his face as we're chatting."

So if you're a guy approaching a woman, keep a respectful distance until signs indicate that you may proceed. And even then, it can't hurt to ask if it's OK to move to the chair next to her. (Not that women don't need to show respect for boundaries, too. "The things that really turn me off are close talkers and loud talkers," one guy wrote.)

Once you're past whatever superficial opening line you've come up with, you might want to blast past chitchat to something at least semi-substantive pretty quickly. You know how introverts feel about chitchat. Talking about the weather won't get you far. Try asking an opinion about something in your immediate surroundings. Introverts have a lot of opinions because we spend a lot of time thinking about stuff. And even if we don't have an opinion already formed on the subject, that sort of question causes us to ponder why we don't have an opinion and whether we should have an opinion and what that opinion might be if we did have one. And that can be a conversational ride in itself.

As an initial conversation comes to an end, you should have a pretty good idea whether it will be appropriate to try taking the acquaintance further by asking for a name, a phone number, or an email address. If you're the kind of person who carries business cards, you can ask to swap cards. Asking for an email address is also an option; email is pretty unthreatening because it keeps communication at arm's length. You can pad the request: "I found a really interesting article about (fascinating subject you just discussed in depth). I'd be glad to send it to you if you give me an email address." Or, more candidly, "I enjoyed talking to you; would you consider swapping email addresses?" Or even, "I'd be happy if you would friend me on Facebook." Asking other people to friend you is less pushy than saying you want to friend them; it gives them an out. If you get a last name, however, you can always try finding and friending the person later and see what happens.

Even better, if you've had the kind of conversation introverts are wont to have—that is to say, real conversation about real things—perhaps you can pick out a common interest around which you might reconnect. "There's a great show at the museum this month; I'll email you if you think you might like to go. . . ." or "I have an extra ticket to (event that you may or may not have tickets to at the moment but could easily get). Would you like to go?"

If the person agrees to whatever, then high fives all round. If not, give yourself big props for trying and get on with your life.

Just Show Up

How to Hit On an Extrovert

Want to meet an extrovert? Piece of cake: Just put yourself in his or her line of sight and look open to conversation. Nick M., a 31-year-old air force medic, insists he wasn't even trying to make a love connection when he started talking to the extrovert who is now his wife. He was visiting her base to conduct some training, and while waiting behind her in the cafeteria line, he asked her what was good. She took it from there. "When I got back to my desk, she emailed me," he says. "In the military, we have our names right there on our clothes. That woman's sneaky, I tell you what."

Sneaky, but smooth. Her motto for the year, Nick says, was, "It's 2009, I'm gonna get mine." Mission accomplished.

Ray-Mel met an interesting extroverted woman at a party just briefly before she went dashing off with friends to another party. But she noticed him and asked the party's hosts about him. "I don't think in a million years I would have asked about anybody," Ray-Mel said. Thank goodness for extroverts—because she asked, the mutual friends made sure the two reconnected at another party, and they clicked.

Actually, his wife's extroversion helped Ray-Mel out at that second meeting, too. "I said, 'Tell me about yourself,' and she got going," Ray-Mel remembers. He barely had to come up with any conversation at all—and he was fine with that. Although, adorably, they were both careful not to trap the other. "She said, 'If you want to talk to other people, you can,'" Ray-Mel remembers. "And I said, 'Well, no. I talk to them all the time. I want to talk to you.'" Good answer, Ray-Mel. Introverts have their own style of smooth moves.

And Laura, who says someone has to practically fall in her lap before she notices them, practically met her extroverted boyfriend that way—although she was closer to being in his lap. It was a Peter Gabriel concert, where she sat in front of him on bench seating at the Santa Barbara Bowl. "His knees were in my back," she says. Laura's daughter had already given her an elbow to the ribs to point out the good-looking guy giving her an interested once-over, but he was the one who made sure to make eye contact and he made the first move. "I was petrified when we met," Laura says. Fortunately for her, he was not.

Score one for meeting extroverts; they make it easy.

With an extrovert, you can start the conversation any old way, without any concern about sounding deep, or thoughtful, or even interesting. One reason introverts find small talk so stressful is that we have trouble letting it be small; we feel we've failed when we hear banalities coming out of our mouths. But remember: That's why they call it small talk. It's small. It's a connection, not a conversation, though you hope it may lead to one. And extroverts in particular understand this, so they won't judge. They'll just dive right in if you make yourself available.

I actually met Drew at a literary event I attended with a friend. I don't remember how we got talking, but I do know he initiated the conversation. Drew is an introvert with smooth party moves; he has a whole small-talk technique for gatherings. He says that rather than walking up to people and introducing himself, he'll wander up to a group and stand and listen. "If within thirty seconds you can tell it's a pretty private conversation, just move on." Otherwise, he says, the trick is to be an active listener: "You don't have to say much. People really like you if you show an interest in them. And if somebody mentions, for example, studying abroad in Spain, I might say, 'My sister lives in Spain; what did you like about it?' Ask, don't talk. If in the first five things you say, more than half are questions, that's good. If the people aren't receptive and give one-word answers, find another group."

And if the whole idea makes you nervous, consider this: "If there are six people in a group, you don't need to do more than one-sixth of the talking," Drew says. "That really relieves pressure."

Take that as flip-side advice, too, especially if you're the kind of introvert who, once uncorked on a subject that interests you, can hold forth for many, many, many sentences. I've had my mouth run away with me on occasion. It happens. So be sure that as you talk, you are also paying attention to the people around you. If you notice eyes are wandering, rein yourself in. I have, on occasion, realized I was blathering and stopped midsentence to save myself by asking a question. Maybe catching myself in a faux pas was obvious to people around me, but if so, all they noticed is that I was trying not to be boorish. Surely all they can do is respect that.

Remember that with extroverts, you never have to wonder or worry if they want to meet a new person—they love meeting new people, never too many, the more the merrier. So approach them as boldly as you please—and don't be afraid, because they'll think nothing of it. Catch 'em at the food table: "Hey, I love your shirt!" or "Did I hear you say you're from Kansas City?" or "Do you think spinach dip counts as a vegetable?" Make eye contact, smile, and then just let the extrovert run with it. See where it goes.

Oh, and by the way, if the whole thing winds up without the extrovert asking for your phone number or email address, then you go ahead and do the asking. Be casual about it, catch the extrovert's arm as he or she dances across the room to wherever, and just toss it out there like it's something you do all the time. "Hey, I'm outta here, but I enjoyed talking to you. Let me give you my business card." Or maybe, "How 'bout an email address?"

Even if the extrovert happily swaps contact info with you, you might end up having to make the next move anyway, since you might be just one of a number of brand-new best friends the extrovert made that week. A quick note or text reminding them where you met and suggesting meeting at another event they might enjoy is a low-stress way of reconnecting; they will let you know if you made the kind of impression you hope for. Again, don't be shy. Extroverts are all about new friends and they're always glad to hear from you.

Fear Not the First Date

Strategies for Easing the Anxiety
of the First Time Out

Let's begin with some slow-start-but-happily-ever-after first-date tales, to prove that even stumbling when you take your first step doesn't mean you're not on the path to love.

When Rebecca got in touch with that guy hugging a horse in a photo on eHarmony, she had five dogs, ten cats, and three parrots. Which tended to intimidate her dates.

Ed and Rebecca emailed awhile, and one Saturday Rebecca complained that she was getting a headache from the racket of having her back deck rebuilt. Ed suggested they meet. This was unusual for him; usually he emailed quite a while longer before suggesting an actual face-to-face meeting.

They decided on an early dinner and Ed went to Rebecca's house to pick her up. The minute he arrived, he was mobbed by Rebecca's pack of large-ish dogs. "He got on the floor, greeted them all, and pretty much forgot about me," Rebecca says. When he realized what he was doing, Ed was sure he had blown the date. "But when he turned to look at me, my face was beaming," Rebecca says.

Call it a sign from dog.

A little more than a year later, they were married.

On Anne's first date with her husband, also an introvert, he talked for five solid hours, mostly about himself. Anne swore she wouldn't be seeing *him* again. "But he called and said, 'Even ballplayers deserve three strikes. You should give me another chance.'" And so she did, figuring that after fifteen years in the navy, he didn't have a lot of game. She did, however, point out his yammerhead faux pas, and the next date he arrived with a list of twenty-six questions to ask Anne about herself. "I thought it was adorably clueless. I never dated anybody else after him," she says.

They've been married twenty-one years.

Kristen met her now-husband at church. They had known each other awhile, but not well, when he asked her on a date. She was reluctant to go out with him; the marked differences in their personalities worried her. "He is a very outgoing and outspoken person and I am *so* not like that." She went on the date, but it did not allay her fears. Although he was immediately smitten, Kristen remained overwhelmed and intimidated by his extroverted ebullience, and for weeks after that ignored his calls and texts. But he wouldn't take no response for an answer. He eventually wore her down and she agreed to a second date. "We met for coffee and realized that under our different personalities, we had a lot of common ground," Kristen says. "I guess it just seemed to finally 'click' for me. And I remember asking him about our different personalities that day and his response was along the lines of needing a balance. He felt that his previous relationship had failed because they were too much alike and it drove him crazy. Go figure."

Now they're newlyweds. Go figure indeed.

Some first dates are neither wonderful nor terrible. Doug M.'s first date with his wife was so-so—nothing special, but good enough to warrant a second date. And even that date started kind of *meh* until a couple of hours in, when the bar where they were started a trivia contest. They joined in, and with that shared effort, they clicked. "We saw that we really worked well together and it wasn't just 'so where are you from?' and 'how many siblings do you have?'" Doug says.

So, first dates are not really the make-or-break events we fear them to be. Despite the high anxiety with which people anticipate them, the dates themselves are often pleasantly forgettable. A lot of the introverts I talked to who are in relationships couldn't recall anything special about their first dates. They went for sushi, they went for pizza, they saw a movie, the conversation was easy. "It was one of the least awkward 'first date' experiences I'd had," says Julie. "He was really easy to talk to, didn't try to be funny or sound smarter than me or talk about himself too much."

"One of the problems I have with extroverts is that they ask so many questions that I feel like I'm being interrogated," says Doug H. "I don't remember feeling like I was being interrogated even though she was doing all of the talking."

I have just a sketchy memory of my first date with my husband. We went to see the movie *Mona Lisa*, then we got a hamburger.

Partway through our meal he asked (with what I would come to know was characteristic bluntness), "So is this a good date? Are you having fun?" I thought that was pretty cute. And yes, I told him, it was and I was.

The moral of all these first-date stories: Don't sweat that first date too much. It might be magic, it might be just OK, it might kinda stink. Ultimately, what is supposed to happen will probably happen regardless of how that first date plays out. The best thing you can do on a first date is go into it with a "what the hell" attitude. Unless (heaven forbid) you are on a date with a sociopath, the worst that can happen is you'll spend a tedious evening. Or maybe you won't make the impression you would hope to make, but as Anne's and Kristen's stories bear out, even that isn't necessarily irreparable.

Drew says that his first dates always go really well. "Usually for me first dates are two, three, four hours long at a restaurant. We usually end up looking at our watches and saying, 'Wow, is it that late?'"

Part of Drew's ease may be because he isn't in any rush to get married—he's ambivalent about the whole idea, actually—and goes into first dates without feeling a lot of pressure, which is bound to take any edge off his experience and behavior. And nothing puts someone else at ease like being at ease yourself. So as you prepare for a first date, put your head in a "let's see what happens" place. Dress appropriately and comfortably rather than to impress. Keep your expectations realistic, if not low. This is a person with whom you are going to spend a few hours, not the rest of your life.

The big plus of first dates for introverts: They're usually one-on-

one, a situation in which we're generally pretty comfortable. And dates are a perfect showcase for our superior listening skills—as long as we don't listen so well that we end up buried in our date's words.

Although, of course, babble is one of those things that can happen to anyone who's nervous. Introverts, who aren't comfortable being the center of attention, might be particularly at risk (as Anne's husband experienced), and we can be mortified when we realize we are dominating the conversation. Many extroverts, on the other hand, don't seem the least bit self-conscious about holding the floor for more than their share of time. But keep in mind that "I'm nervous" is not a terrible thing to say if you find yourself skidding out of control in any way on a date—careening off into babble, spilling your water glass, taking a wrong turn en route to the restaurant. Any nice person will empathize. One psychological study even suggests that people find embarrassment endearing. Remember, too, that your date is probably equally nervous, so try not to judge harshly if he or she acts weird in some way. Instead, chalk it up to nervousness and see if that puts the weirdness in a different light.

If a first date is only so-so—neither dazzling nor disastrous—a second date is probably a good idea. Everyone has an off night now and then, so if you're still intrigued after one date, give it another try. First dates are just experiments. They're exploratory.

The key thing to remember is that you can never, ever, ever go wrong by just being who you are, warts and babbles and awkward blurts and all. You never know what will endear you to the right person.

For Best Results, Make a Plan

Setting the Stage for a Good First Date

Before sticking your neck out and asking someone for a date, you'll want to formulate a plan. Asking someone to "go out sometime" sounds wishy-washy and noncommittal, and like "sometime" might never happen. It gives you an out, whether you want it or not. And while an extrovert might jump right in and make you pin the invitation down, an introvert might be less aggressive. In addition, it's easy for another person to agree to something nebulous while thinking, "Not a chance—I'll just beg off when the real invitation arrives," giving you false hope. So if you really want that date to happen, get specific. Produce a plan of sorts—something concrete but with wiggle room to negotiate.

And if you're on the receiving end of the invitation, don't go all mushy and acquiescent, mumbling "whatever you want to do." Say yes or no to the idea presented, suggest an alternative if you're interested in the person but not the activity, and negotiate the date you want.

A few reasons this is a good idea: You can learn how flexible/ open-minded/agreeable the person is in a negotiation, you can learn early if the two of you enjoy spending time the same way, and you have a better chance of having a good time on a date if you're doing something you enjoy. So stand your ground. Don't say yes to an Adam Sandler movie if you prefer Ingmar Bergman. Don't agree to rock climbing if heights give you a stomachache. Don't plan to visit an art museum if you're more the NASCAR kind. Sure, if the relationship "takes," then you'll want to explore each other's interests, but for the first date, common ground helps ensure everyone is comfortable.

Here are pros, cons, and caveats for some first-date ideas:

Movies: I've heard different opinions about movies for a first date, since you can't talk and get to know each other during a film. Still, dinner and a movie are a classic first date—although if you're a slow-to-warm introvert, you might reverse the order and see the movie first, so you'll be ready for conversation by the time you're sitting across a table from your date.

PROS: A nice concrete invitation—it's an easy segue from a get-to-know-you conversation to suggesting a movie relevant to the topic, and any negotiation provides insight into the other person's tastes and interests. Movies are more affordable than concerts or theater, and are a springboard for conversation afterward.

CONS: You spend two hours of your date sitting silently and wondering if your date is enjoying the film.

CAVEATS: Avoid anything raunchy or with a lot of nudity and sex; watching that kind of stuff with someone you don't know well can be mighty uncomfortable. Think about a movie you wouldn't mind seeing with your mother and save the more adult themes for when you're better acquainted.

Meals: A meal is another classic date, and a natural add-on to any other activity. A lot of getting-to-know-you stuff can happen over the dining table, both intentionally and unintentionally. Remember Diane Keaton ordering pastrami on white with mayo in *Annie Hall*? (Never seen it? It includes some of filmdom's most excruciatingly insightful early-dating scenes.)

    PROS: This is the kind of socializing introverts like best, where you can focus on the person and conversation without a lot of distractions (unless you have one of those annoying waiters who checks in every two minutes). Also, you can learn a lot about a person by how he or she treats service people. Is she rude to the waiter? Check, please.

    CONS: "Do I have spinach in my teeth?" Also, if the date doesn't go well, a meal can seem mighty long.

    CAVEATS: This isn't the least bit fair, but a friend once went on a date with a woman who ordered an egg salad sandwich, and he was so turned off by watching her eat it, he couldn't bring himself to ask for a second date. I know, I know. But I'm just passing along the hard facts.

    Rebecca has another caveat. "I have extensive food allergies, so I often end up being forced to order exceptionally healthy when

I'd much rather eat a giant bacon cheeseburger," she says. "Every first date I had, the guy ordered the exact thing I did and it was really annoying. It seemed terribly false. They couldn't have really wanted the fish and steamed vegetables."

Also, women, don't offer to split the tab and then get secretly pissed if he lets you. I mean, really . . . Offer or don't offer, but don't set a trap.

Museums: A museum date is oh-so-introvertish. It's all quiet and arty (or historical or science-y) and chatter is not encouraged, so your tendency to choose your words carefully and sparingly won't be at all out of place.

PROS: Looking at art with other people provides a glimpse of their soul. History museums let you see their depth of knowledge. Also, big museums have great places to sit and people-watch. When I visit New York City, an old friend and I always go to the Metropolitan Museum of Art. We look at some art, then we find a spot to sit and people-watch and catch up. (It's a busy enough spot that our conversation is not distracting to others.)

CONS: You and your date might have vastly different tastes in art and you risk getting judgmental with each other.

CAVEATS: It's easy to sound like a pretentious windbag talking about art. Try not to do that.

Hiking, biking, or other outdoor activity: If you're the kind of person who likes this kind of thing, then you might want to find the kind of person who also likes this kind of thing. (Unless you use this kind of thing as a way to escape other people, in which case never mind what I just said.)

PROS: Get those endorphins going and your date might look even better than before. Plus, even if the date doesn't work out, you get your workout in. Also, conversation is not required all the time. You can talk, you can not talk, it's all good.

CONS: One of you might be faster, stronger, more adept than the other, which could conceivably lead to someone feeling bad.

CAVEATS: This is not the time to be competitive. Treat it like a team sport and you're both on the same team. And for heaven's sake, unless it's specifically requested, don't coach. If nobody asked for your advice, then just don't. It's annoying.

Flea market/street fair: Again, if you like this sort of thing, it's inexpensive and there's lots to look at and talk about.

PROS: They're usually free, so if you decide you'd rather go someplace and talk, no loss. And if you're shy or worried about what you'll find to talk about at first, lots of stuff to look at gives you lots of stuff to talk about. Maybe there will be music, maybe jugglers, maybe face painting for kids (not to jump the gun, but that's an entrée to sussing out each other's attitudes about procreating). You also can assess each other's tastes and interests. Do you share similar taste in art, or is one drawn to paintings of bluebonnets while the other prefers contemporary geometrics? Are you both collectors? Do you both love rummaging through boxes of old record albums? When you get tired of looking at stuff, you can find someplace to perch and watch, always fun for introverts.

CONS: Some introverts find crowds difficult to cope with, so if things start getting tight, you might have to explain yourself and request a change of venue. And while this might be a pro or a con, depending on how you feel about it, an extrovert might find it necessary to chitchat up every vendor in the place.

CAVEATS: Don't treat this as an opportunity for serious shopping. If you find some perfectly wonderful something, go ahead. But save serious shopping for when you're alone or with a good friend so that your attention isn't drawn away from your date.

Walk in the park or an interesting neighborhood: A person who is happy just meandering and doesn't always need to be doing something specific can be an awfully nice person to hang around with.

PROS: Side-by-side conversation can be more relaxed than face-to-face conversation, and having lots going on takes some pressure off you to be fascinating. Also, lulls in the conversation aren't as awkward when you're strolling. And when you're ready to really concentrate on each other, you can find a bench or café and settle in.

CONS: This kind of date doesn't have an obvious end point, like a movie, a meal, or even a museum visit. So if you're not having a grand time, you might have to do the old, "Oh, gosh, look at the time . . ." thing to escape.

CAVEATS: The lack of a specific activity has the potential for some awkwardness before the conversation gets rolling.

Whatever sounds fun to both of you can potentially work for a first date, but consider some of the drawbacks to these activities that may or may not make for a comfortable first time out:

Live music at a club: Lots of fun if you have similar tastes in music, but tough for conversation.

Wedding: Not unless you're cool with a lot of awkward questions.

Family event: Same as above, plus the possibility of TMI too fast as either you or your date (depending on whose event it is) interacts with family.

Theater or concert: Fine if ticket prices are reasonable, but a little risky if they're a splurge and you think you might resent your date if he or she isn't bowled over by the experience.

Party or other group activity: Introverts don't compete for airspace very well and you might fade into the background if there's a lot of extrovert hubbub.

Bar: Great for conversation as long as you can pace your drinking.

Truth in Advertising

Putting Your Introversion Out There

A while back I received a note from a woman married to a man she met in college. They did a lot of running around and partying in their college days. You know how that is. But then, after they graduated and got married, she settled comfortably into a homebody introvert life. She found it "hilarious," she said, that her husband was puzzled by her sudden change. "I don't think he realized at the time that he was marrying an introvert," she wrote.

No, he probably didn't and I feel kinda bad for him. I'm sure she didn't do it intentionally, but it's kind of interpersonal bait and switch, isn't it?

Granted, only in recent years has anybody given much thought to introversion and extroversion and the implications they have for our relationships. Most of us were too busy trying to be—or at least pretending to be—extroverts, since we were told that extroverts were happier and more successful, and less weird and pathetic.

In fact, if the emails and blog comments I've received over the years are any indication, a lot of introverts didn't even realize they were introverts; they just thought there was something wrong with them. The relief that comes through in many of the messages I receive is practically palpable.

But now that we are thinking about our introversion, accepting it, and figuring out what it means for the way we live, we can start consciously factoring it into our relationships. Sure, each of us is a complex combination of traits, experiences, characteristics, and quirks but—speaking very generally—our introversion implies that we have a certain number of shared needs and quirks, and it makes sense to take those into consideration as we embark on new relationships.

"Know thyself" and "like thyself" aren't exactly groundbreaking revelations in the pursuit of a good relationship, and certainly there's a whole lot more about yourself you'll want to know and like beyond your introversion. But as you become familiar with yourself as an introvert, you also want to make sure your potential partner understands the impact this facet of your personality will have on your relationship.

Early in our relationship, I told my husband that I didn't believe couples needed to be joined at the hip. He seemed slightly taken aback at the moment, but as it happens, he's a pretty independent dude himself and we never did have any significant friction over the issue. In fact, he might have just never considered the possibility that alone time was OK in the context of a relationship.

A lot of us assume that being in a relationship means spending

every possible moment together; this is something our culture en-
courages. Beth admits that early in her relationship, she fretted over
the time her now-husband needed to himself, afraid that it signaled
something was amiss. But with maturity, she says, came a different
perspective. "I started to see the value of true alone time," she says.
"I also think I was finally starting to figure out who I was as an
individual."

Figuring yourself out is, of course, the first order of business,
and learning your partner's needs is a close second. If you've lived
in such a way that you have been able to fully indulge your introversion, keeping to yourself more than not, then another person's
needs might be a bit of a learning curve. At the time he met his
wife-to-be at an educational workshop in Denver, David was living
in a Buddhist community in a small village in England. He had
been there so long that it didn't really occur to him that his ascetic
life—no radio, television, CD player—wouldn't appeal to everyone.
When his new girlfriend came for a visit, "For some reason—and
this sounds kind of awkward—I didn't think about taking her out
and about. I thought there was enough there," he says. "And she
got more than restless—I think she planned to take the next plane
back to the States."

Fortunately, he figured it out soon enough. After six years of
marriage, though, they're still adjusting. David is still not sure his
wife really gets the concept of introversion. He tried unsuccessfully
to persuade her to read books or articles about it, but ultimately,
in his Buddhist way, decided not to force the issue.

Doug H. and his now-wife confronted the issues explicitly. She commented on his introverted tendencies, they talked it out, and adjusted accordingly—spending more time with small groups than large, for example, which accommodated both their preferences. Then, after they were married, Doug attended a leadership conference for work that required him to take the Myers-Briggs personality inventory, which he found very enlightening. He had his wife and kids take the online version shortly after that. Twenty-eight years married now, Doug and his wife still meet in the middle when it comes to socializing. "We intentionally try to have other activities with groups," he says. "We're very active at our church, so there are events that feed the extrovert in her. And it's a small group, so I'm comfortable."

When they were starting to get serious, Brett and his girlfriend had to work out some friction over what he describes as her "reliance on friends for happiness." He says, "Even as we began dating, she had a hard time putting her friends on the back burner to make time for us. I got feisty and impatient. The only thing that solved it, really, was her coming around to trusting that I could make her as happy and comfortable as her friends. She is still close with her friends, but she no longer relies on them."

For the most part, issues and adjustments related to introversion tend to unfold organically over the course of dating and getting to know each other. You can help it all along by not making an issue of your introvert needs, but simply mentioning them as a matter of course. "A big party like that doesn't really sound like my kind of thing. I'll go if you really want me to, but I also don't mind if you go without me." Or "I might have had enough of this event after an hour or so. Would you like to take two cars, in case you want to stay longer?" Or "I've had people talking at me all week. I'm really looking forward to an evening of silence and solitude on the couch."

But even as you are setting necessary boundaries, you want to be sure you're not erecting walls. I've received a few heartbreaking notes from people who feel shut out by their introverted mates. One woman said that after their children left home, she turned one of their bedrooms into a man cave for her husband, then regretted it when he started spending most of his time in it. "I have been studying about introverts and still feel so inadequate with my husband!" she wrote. "I am an extrovert. I have through the years become somewhat reclusive because of him. (Who wants to always be going places without your better half?) He has gotten worse because we have no one living at home to interact with him. I have learned to give him his space and in so doing probably added to his introvertness!"

Don't be that guy. But don't be someone you aren't, either. Hiding your introversion is a bad idea because introversion itself is not a problem. It only causes problems if different needs aren't factored into a burgeoning relationship and handled with respect and understanding. No doubt introversion-related issues will come up over time in a long-term relationship—healthy relationships are fluid and ever changing—but if you start out being honest with yourself and the other person, you will have built a foundation for later adaptation, compromise, and mutual comfort and happiness. With no awkward surprises.

Use Your Words!

What to Say When You Need Some Space

It's all very well to say that as introverts we are entitled to live as we choose, but sometimes the words we need in order to set boundaries without causing offense don't roll easily off our tongues. So we stammer justifications and fumble with excuses and often end up acquiescing to whatever others want because we just can't find solid ground to stand on.

What is that solid ground? You need what you need, and when you need solitude/to go home/to say no or any other boundary, nobody should be able to convince you differently.

Sure, a little white lie now and then can do the trick when you need to stake out some space, but the upside of telling the truth about your introverted needs is that the more you are honest about them, the more people learn to understand and the more accustomed they get to letting you have your space.

So herewith are some suggestions for the words to use for various situations:

No plans for me tonight, thanks. Is your new squeeze trying to get you to commit to fun, fun, fun when what you really want is quiet, quiet, quiet? Don't make up previous commitments. Tell the truth: "It's not you, it's me." You need downtime. The other person can try to argue, but you know you best; don't let anyone throw you.

Try saying:

- I'm going on lockdown for some "me" time this weekend.
- It's been a long day. I need a TV couch party tonight.
- Can I take a rain check? I'm due for a quiet evening/weekend.

The party's over, I'm going home. You went to the party, you had a nice time at the party, now you would like to leave the party. "Oh nooooooo," your date and your friends all wail. "You have to stay! We're just getting started! You'll miss the best part!"

First of all, no, you won't. It will almost certainly just be more of the same, only with less food. Second, when you're done, you're done. Remember: It's a lot easier to say yes to invitations if you let yourself bail out when you've had enough.

Try saying:

- I've had all the fun I can handle for one night.
- I've given it everything I've got. I have nothing left.

- I need to go before I embarrass myself by falling asleep on the couch.

The more isn't the merrier for me. Sometimes an invitation to a group event sounds fun. Most of us know when an invitation sounds all wrong for us, however, even if it's from someone we really like. Often it's the event, not the person, we want to decline.

Try saying:

- I'm not feeling up to a group right now.
- It sounds fun but I prefer to spend some time with just the two of us.
- I'm going to skip this one; it doesn't sound like my kind of thing.
- I think you'll have more fun without having to concern yourself with whether I'm having fun, so why don't you do this one without me?

I really, really, really need to back out of this plan. I do not advocate backing out of plans willy-nilly—especially if the plan is with just one other person (as opposed to a group, where you might be missed but you won't derail things altogether). Backing out frequently is rude and unkind. The people who really care about us, however, will give us get-out-of-plans-free cards now and then, when we really need it. Just use them sparingly and thoughtfully. (And, needless to say, no backing out because you got a better offer, unless that better offer is restorative solitude.)

Try saying:

- Would you hate me if I beg off tonight? I'm in dire need of not doing anything.
- Would I leave you high and dry if I ask for a rain check?
- I promise I'll be a lot more fun if we can reschedule this for another day, when I have more energy.

Pay attention to how your new beau responds when you need to use these words. Understanding? Resentful? Supportive? Irritated? These are important clues. At the same time, pay attention to how often you need to use these words. If you find yourself having to trot them out frequently, then consider that you might be in an ill-fitting relationship with someone who needs more time/attention/action than you have to give. No judgment, just something to consider before you're in too deep.

Red Flag, Red Flag, Red Flag!

Sometimes It's Best to Just Walk Away

There are problems, and then there are problems. There are problems that might require some squabbling, some hurt feelings, some heartfelt discussion, some compromise and change, but that can ultimately be worked out. But other issues might show themselves in repeating patterns that are more than just problems—they're red flags that you might be embarking on an unsuitable relationship. It's easy to be blinded by infatuation, or convinced you are being too sensitive (something a lot of introverts have heard all their lives), or you might simply be missing out on important input from other people.

In some ways, introverts are like sponges. We soak up what is happening around us. Because we are such good listeners and sensitive to the vibes of people around us, we are ultra-tuned in to the needs of others. Like anyone else, we want to be liked and appreciated, but because we are reserved and don't draw a lot of attention to ourselves, we might have a tendency to offer ourselves up as sounding boards and to anticipate others' needs and sublimate our own for the connections we crave. Or we might be ashamed of our introversion and try to quash it to meet the demands of people around us.

"My introversion, which from an early age was not seen as 'normal,' led me into trying to be more of an extrovert," says John. "Long story short, it led to subverting my needs to others and not advocating for my needs, to resenting that eventually, and to a distance between us that could not be repaired. Fundamentally, my inability to be myself, and feel comfortable with who I was, led to marrying someone who was not a good match."

Mismatches are sad, but other introvert-related relationship mistakes can even be scary. After one of her relationships turned bad and she broke it off, Melissa had an unnerving epiphany. "Introversion makes it easier to become isolated or manipulated into a bad relationship," she cautions. "When we'd both rather spend the night in and I never brought him around my friends, there's a big missing puzzle piece of social interaction and necessary feedback from outside observers about a relationship dynamic."

Like many introverts, Melissa tends to keep to herself and trusts herself to work out her own problems, so there was nobody else keeping watch over her relationship who might throw up a red flag about troubling patterns of behavior—"problems I couldn't quite—or wouldn't—see," she says.

So before you get in too deep, turn on your introvert superpowers of perception and consult your closest friends to see if something that feels uncomfortable might actually be a big-deal problem. You might save yourself some heartache down the line by either changing the relationship dynamic, or deciding it is not a relationship you can thrive in.

Here are some red flags to keep a lookout for, and if you see one waving, proceed with caution:

The "Oh, OK" red flag: Does your new squeeze have awesome powers of persuasion? Do you find yourself saying (aloud or to yourself), "Oh, OK" to one more social event, one more family gathering, one more whatever it is that you really don't have the energy for but don't have the energy to fight? Does this person wheedle and beg when you try to say no until "Oh, OK" just seems like the easiest way to put an end to the fuss? Red flag! If you can't say no, if the other person won't let you say no without an argument, you may be setting yourself up for a life of perpetual exhaustion and probably eventual resentment. Either learn to say no and mean it, or accept that this person might not be your love match.

The previous chapter suggested some noninflammatory ways to say no. After you do, you have to just hold peacefully to your decision through any guilt trips or hissy fits that might be aimed your way. If you can't do that, or if your partner works you until you finally give in, a red flag is waving.

Of course, you also want to be sure that you don't act overtly or passive aggressively neglected should your partner go do these things without you. Which leads me to another red flag . . .

The "What's the point?" red flag: Feeling neglected? Seems like your partner always has something going on? Not getting enough attention when you're out in a group? Feeling like you have to beg for one-on-one time? Do you wonder what's the point of being in a relationship when you have to fend for yourself so often? You might not be in a love match. That's not to say the other person's needs are wrong and that yours are right, or vice versa. Needs are needs and everyone's job is to recognize their own needs and honor them. You get to honor your needs, but so does the other person. So if your honey needs a lot more action than you do—or a lot more solitude, if he or she is further down the introversion continuum than you—and you don't feel like you're getting enough from your relationship, first try honest discussion, and if that doesn't lead to change you can both live with, consider that you might be better off as friends.

The "Got a better idea?" red flag: Often when someone wants us to do something, even if we don't really want to, we tell ourselves—or the other person may imply— "Well, it's not like I have anything better to do. . . ." And sometimes that's true. But sometimes you do have something better to do, which just happens to be nothing.

Historically, psychologists have looked at introversion as the absence of extroversion. They measure extroversion, and if you are low in it, then you are considered an introvert. This perpetuates the perception of introversion as negative space, and introverted activities as not really doing anything. We need to train ourselves, and others, out of this idea. We need to start seeing doing nothing (or reading, or working alone on projects, or whatever it is we do to recharge) as activities that are as valid as any social event. If you frequently find yourself dressing to go out when you'd planned an evening in sweatpants, you might be giving your own needs the short shrift and setting yourself up for some hard times ahead.

The "Try it, you'll like it" red flag: First the disclaimer: Trying new things is great. It keeps us vital and engaged with the world, it pushes us out of our comfort zone, and it makes us grow as human beings.

That said, after we reach a certain age, we have a pretty good idea of what sounds fun and what sounds hellish. For example, I love yoga and I enjoy trying different yoga classes. But there's something called laughter yoga that I'm not going to try, thankyouverymuch. No, really. I won't like it. Call me small-minded and stubborn, but don't tell me I don't know my own mind.

A person who is constantly trying to push you into things you don't want to do may have trouble respecting boundaries. This is certainly not an issue for introverts alone, but since many of us have heard for so long that our introversion is wrong, we may be trained to question and perhaps dismiss our own preferences, leading us to believe what others tell us we should and should not enjoy. Just remember that nobody knows you better than you. If something really, truly, no kidding around doesn't sound like fun, then you are not obligated to try it.

So, as long as we are otherwise pushing ourselves in ways that sound interesting and toward the kinds of growth we want, then we are perfectly justified in sometimes saying, "No, I won't like it," and leaving it at that. No matter how hard your sweetie insists that if you would only just *try* . . .

The "Three's company" red flag: Do you get enough just-the-two-of-you time, or does the extrovert you love like an entourage everywhere you go? Nobody should have to sacrifice their friends for a relationship, but you probably want your sweetheart to enjoy quiet time just with you as well. If it seems like plans always include friends, it might be time for a little talk. And if that leads to accusations that you're antisocial or don't like people or are too needy, run like hell.

The inverse of this is that if you're more comfortable with your partner when you're around other people, if you feel like you're not enough and that having other people around takes the pressure off you, maybe you're selling yourself short or have connected to someone who doesn't reflect back to you your best self. An intimate relationship is no place to be a shrinking violet.

The "Did you say something?" red flag: Introverts are great listeners and we pride ourselves on that. We also pride ourselves on choosing our words carefully and not speaking unless we have something to say. Both are fine qualities that I admire, but I've also found myself in relationships where I've done all the listening. One of my less-than-admirable qualities is that I like feeling wise. It's my own little power trip to be the one to whom people come with their problems. But eventually I hit a listening wall and realize a relationship has become imbalanced, that I have sublimated my own need to be heard to my need for that very special type of oh-so-wise power. And then I get resentful and blame the other person. Everybody loses.

The fact is, though, that I have to force myself to speak up when it comes to my own needs. This isn't all about introversion—it's a mishmash of all sorts of things about my personality and past—but because my comfort zone is listening, as it is for so many introverts, I can easily sink into a sort of complacent receptor mode. This isn't fair to me and it isn't fair to the people in my life, including my husband, who shouldn't be left to guess my needs. So next time you think keeping your thoughts to yourself is doing your relationship a favor, think again, to be sure.

The "Everything is fine" red flag: We'll get further into this later, in the chapter on conflict, but two careful introverts who connect but then try to avoid conflict and confrontation at all costs are likely to end up in a relationship precariously perched on eggshells. No relationship is perfect, and resisting all conflict is not the same as never having any. In fact, relationship expert John Gottman does much of his research into marriage by looking at the ways couples handle conflict. If they do it well, the relationship will have legs. If not, he predicts (usually correctly) failure. And refusing to engage in healthy conflict is not a good sign.

The "Let's not bother" red flag: So far I've talked about ways extroverts might try to push you to do more than you want. But an introvert-introvert relationship risk is frequently talking yourselves out of doing things you had planned to do. This, alas, is a bit of a problem in my own marriage: We see something that looks fun and have every intention of getting out and doing it, but then the time comes and we both sort of go limp and wait for the other to motivate us both out of the house. "How badly do you want to go?" we ask each other, and if neither one of us jumps up to cheerlead the idea, we allow inertia to make the decision.

So what's the problem? If neither of you wanted to do it, why do it? Well, because often we wake up the next morning and one or both of us kick ourselves because we really *did* want to do whatever it was, but the inertia of two people was more than we could transcend. If you find that you frequently talk each other out of having a life *and regret it* (key point), then maybe you are two introverts bringing out the worst in each other.

"Run away, run away!" (more than a red flag): Quite a few of the introverts I've talked to for this book said that they are rarely, if ever, the pursuers in relationships. Because narcissistic people can be predatory, seeking out passive souls who might bend to their will, and because some introverts can be passive about letting relationships come to them, it's a good idea to know the red flags of narcissism. Beware the person who needs lots of ego strokes; who considers himself or herself a rare and exceedingly special person that only other rare and exceedingly special people can understand; who lives in a fantasy world of success and power; who expects the world to cede to his or her every wish; who preens in the light of the world's alleged envy. If your new interest displays any of these traits, proceed with caution. Oh, and none of these qualities is exclusive to extroverts; that introvert sitting in a corner passing judgment on everyone around could be a narcissist of a different flavor, no less unpleasant. So if you find the attentions of a gifted charmer turned your way, be sure to look past the dazzle of the love light to be sure it's not blinding you to a dark side.

PART III

The Quiet Way
to Happily Ever After

From Dating to a Relationship

I Love You but Please Don't Call Me

Communicating About Communicating

When counselors and relationship experts talk about communication as the cornerstone of a relationship, they're talking about the ability to express your needs and talk through problems. But these days, with cell phones, texting, and email allowing us to come at each other every which way, communicating about communicating can be an issue in itself—especially in relationships. It's good to begin that conversation about communication preferences early, in order to avoid bigger misunderstandings.

One of the commonalities I've discovered among many, many introverts is a strong dislike for the telephone, which can be a surprisingly hot topic in relationships. Many people seem to think that dislike of the telephone is some sort of moral failing, that it means we dislike the person on the other end of the telephone, that rejecting the medium is rejecting the message. But this is not the case.

Many introverts simply find talking on the phone awkward and prefer almost any form of communication over a telephone call.

One introvert married to an extrovert complained that sometimes his wife will call him five minutes after leaving the house. "I didn't even have any time to enjoy being alone!" he griped in a blog comment. Another woman, also with an extrovert, seconded that emotion: Early in their relationship, her now-husband called her five times a day. It totally got on her nerves.

Shannon, a 34-year-old flight paramedic who is single, says that too much contact in general is probably the quickest way to short-circuit a budding relationship with him. "It seems needy and untrusting and it's a huge red flag for me."

Drew, too, struggles with girlfriends' expectations of daily phone calls. "If I go a whole day and haven't done more than texted, I feel a little bad going to bed. Is she mad at me because I didn't call?"

The telephone is a big communication issue, but there are other ways we can get on each other's nerves with our communication styles. Don tried and tried to be patient with his second wife, who was in constant contact throughout the day while he was at work. "She understood when I had to go but at the same time would get upset with me if I didn't have much to say," he says. "I only have so much to say during the day and I liked to save it until I got home for family time . . . otherwise I would have very little to say and be accused of not wanting to talk."

And, he says, his wife was text happy, sending "endless" texts all day, keeping him apprised of her every move. "Those were easier to deal with, I could keep pace a little better with the conversation and take my time responding, but it was still a struggle sometimes coming up with something more than 'LOL!' as a response to her quips and remarks about what the cats were doing at any given time."

My husband and I also have had to work out communication problems. I've tried his patience by using text and email instead of the telephone. He's not crazy about either, and if I send him a two-sentence email, he often reads just the first sentence, which drives me crazy. He's missed some interesting information that way, like the time the second sentence was about a plumbing emergency. My emails to him have gotten shorter and shorter and sometimes I just put whatever I need to say in the subject line and leave it at that. The other day I texted something or other to him and he responded tersely: "Call me."

All things considered, he prefers the telephone. So I called him.

We've had explicit conversations about all this and have reached an unofficial compromise: After a few back and forths via email or text—to nail down a plan, for example—we take it to the telephone and get 'er done. You give a little, you take a little.

That's not to say that we never screw up—he still sometimes doesn't read my emails, I still text when he would prefer a phone call. But we have discussed the problem enough to be able to short-hand our way out of any squabbles about the matter: "Hey, you know I don't like that . . ." is sufficient.

Of course, you might find that you both enjoy lots of casual text and email contact throughout the day. Tyler and his wife do. "I find I miss it when it doesn't happen," he says, although he's pretty sure that without text, they wouldn't be in touch as much during the day. Brett says he and his fiancée exchange seven to ten emails a day—just little quips or links to stories of interest. "I'd miss her if I didn't hear from her," he says.

Tone and her introverted husband also text a lot during the day—a little more than she needs but she's happy to keep him happy. And, she says, if one of them reads between the lines that something might be wrong on the other side of the communication, they switch to the telephone. "It is easy to discover, even if the other one doesn't write it right out," Tone says.

If you have a mate who likes more contact than you do during the day, maybe you can agree to certain hours when you're open or will respond to texts or phone calls. Blame the boss if you have to, or your own inability to multitask. (Actually, nobody is really good at multitasking; our brains don't work that way.)

Or perhaps a discussion about "guess what the cat did" texts will help. Chances are, the person who sends a lot of those mostly wants a little connection; perhaps if you take the time to say hi during the day, your partner will feel less inclination to provide blow-by-blow reports on feline hijinks. (Or canine. I confess to sometimes reporting our dog's antics to my husband during the workday. Perhaps I should ask him how he feels about that.)

And of course, communication issues aren't all about phone, text, and the like. You can run into them when you're face to face, too. Introverts can be phlegmatic and easily overwhelmed by talkety-talkers.

Don not only had trouble keeping up with both of his former

wives' daily contact in their married days; he became overwhelmed by their need to express themselves . . . and express themselves . . . and express themselves face to face, too. Ultimately the chitchat divide was too great to successfully traverse. "I would try to come up with things to talk about or relay the small, pointless things that had happened at work that day, basically trying to keep my wives happy, as they seemed to think that if I wasn't talking, I was ignoring them or not interested in them," he says. "It was painful at times trying to come up with small talk and I really struggled with it."

He tried talking the matter out with his second wife. "She was getting upset with me to the point where she was claiming I didn't *want* to talk to her," he recalls. "I tried to explain that wasn't the case, that I am not the type of person who talks just for the sake of talking, and if anything exciting happened during my day, she would be the first to know. I also tried to explain that was the reason for the quiet lulls in our conversations, either in person or on the phone. I said what I had to say, and I was done. It wasn't that I didn't want to talk to her or was ignoring her."

Ultimately, Don and his wives weren't able to negotiate compatible communication styles, and while that might not have been the death blow for the marriages, the fact that they couldn't work it out without hurt feelings and misunderstandings was a bad omen—they had problems communicating about communicating, a sort of communication problem squared.

In these types of situations, an outside assessment can help. When my friend Carol Lennox, a psychotherapist in Austin, Texas, sees couples with similar conflicts, she administers a short version of the Myers-Briggs test, right there in her office. "It's free, it's seventy-five questions, and I'll have each person read the other person's while they're sitting there," she says. This, she explains, plants the seeds of understanding and paves the way to concrete strategies, such as agreeing to give each other an hour of unwinding time at the end of the workday before the chatter begins.

As with so many aspects of relationships, sometimes a sense of humor is all you need to make a problem less problematic. "My husband is a chatterbox and I love him, obviously, but he has a nasty habit of starting to talk to me when I am trying to watch a movie, read, or go to bed," one woman wrote. "We have started to have a sense of humor about it," she says—but I'll bet there was some eye-rolling and stifled irritation before they got it out in the open.

Tom and I joke about retreating to our "happy place" in our heads when a monologue continues past our limited attention span for other people's speechifying—including each other's, at times. Yeah, I know, we want to think our loved ones hang on our every word. But sometimes . . . well, you just need to keep a little humility about it. As long as you pay full, loving attention to each other when it really matters, forgive each other for retreating to the happy place sometimes. It's a strategy to use sparingly (or at least very discreetly) with a loved one, but it can be pretty handy.

Modern technology can also provide some help. Turn off your cell phone or put an auto-response on texts when you need to concentrate. If my husband has lots to tell me while I'm watching a show, the pause button on the DVR helps out.

Communication incompatibility is one of those things that usually shakes down over time—one person stops craving constant contact, you both figure out when you're becoming obtrusive or not accessible enough, and you eventually even out to a style that feels comfortable for both.

And while you are within your rights to want your partner to adapt to some degree to your needs, be aware that staying too rigid can become lonely, as one woman reported on my blog. A "super-introverted person" who is attracted to extroverted men, she struggled with the communication thing because she simply doesn't need a lot of interaction. Even though she might think of the person all the time, she said, she can easily coast through a week without contact. "In the beginning this works well, since there is really not much to talk about," she said. "Yet over time, it never fails: The man senses distance and immediately begins to seek attention somewhere else." She now tries to work in lunch or dinner dates during the week, and sends little "love texts" now and then. "Little things that remind my companion that I do consider his feelings."

If you aren't proactive about determining communication preferences, you might find yourself having odd little squabbles, squalls that seem to come out of nowhere over phone calls or text messages. It might seem like the problem is the message, not the mode. But with so many bandwidths of communication, it may actually be less about what you're saying than how and when.

Meet Me on the Couch

A Quiet Kind of Fun

Introvert fun is a quiet kind of fun. We don't always need a lot of action, we certainly don't need a lot of people, and sometimes the smallest, most trivial pastimes make us the happiest. And it can be even better when we can find someone else who likes doing that not-much-of-anything with us.

My husband and I agree that a Sunday spent puttering around the house—newspaper, breakfast, a little housework with music playing, maybe some yardwork, a run to the supermarket, a nice home-cooked dinner—is a fine day and concludes with a feeling of peace and satisfaction.

Some Sundays we enjoy little day trips to a barbecue joint we like, with maybe a stop in a small town for some antiquing. We like going out to dinner, the two of us or with another couple. We like going to hear live music. We like movies. We like outdoor festivals, the State Fair of Texas, and baseball games—places where there are a lot of people, none of whom we are required to talk to.

We like doing a little bit of this, a little bit of that, a lot of nothing in particular, and we like doing it together. After a long workday, we like sitting together in front of the TV. We call it a TV couch party. We have a tradition of going out to dinner on Friday nights; the change of scenery helps us focus on each other after a week of distractions.

Introverts have come up with all sorts of strategies to get through—even enjoy, in our way—the kind of fun extroverts like. But that doesn't mean those things are our first choice for fun, and it's always particularly delightful to find another soul who can quietly enjoy quiet pleasures with us.

Rebecca and Ed are perfectly happy staying home together and doing their own thing, although they do sometimes look up and realize it's been months since they've gone out and about, so they rouse themselves and go. "Even then what we like to do tends to not involve others," says Rebecca. "For our last vacation, we rented a cabin in the mountains and hiked to nearby waterfalls. We like to go to museums, small venue concerts, or star parties and look through the telescopes."

Who says introverts don't party? They star party.

"We both like to stay in and watch movies together," says Melissa. "We both like to take walks when the weather is nice, and to swim together. We occasionally attend parties together, but I've dropped out of attending most of his friends' gatherings, preferring to go to bed early, to get up early and run. He hates running, but every once in a while I can twist his arm."

An extra benefit of dating an introvert: Cheap dates!

"We both enjoy small get-togethers with one or two other couples," says Beth. "And we like to do things together in a crowd, like a movie, baseball game, or concert." Introverts' idea of the more the merrier.

Finding fun common ground isn't hard for introvert-introvert couples. And even if we don't enjoy the same things all the time, since introverts are comfortable doing things alone, going off and doing our own thing is easy when our partner understands—both the need to do it and the fact that we often don't mind doing it. No explanations, no hurt feelings, no guilt trips.

"I'm not much for video games, but he has plenty of friends to play them with, and I have plenty of friends to see musicals and symphonies with," Melissa says. "It's a pleasant balance between shared activities and independence."

Actually, that's a pretty accurate description of an introvert-introvert relationship in general: Shared and independent. We do things together, we do things alone, we do things alone together—in the same house and even the same room, but in our own heads.

Admittedly, I wish my husband enjoyed hiking as much as I do, but since it's not really his thing, I usually go alone or find a friend. I'm OK going to movies on my own, and sometimes actually prefer it; I'd rather go see a talky, slow-moving, full-of-feelings, explosion-free movie by myself than drag him along and spend the entire time wondering exactly how bored he is. (Actually, to be fair,

Tom doesn't really go for explosion-based movies. But he's never met a Mafia flick he didn't like.) And for his part, Tom will go hear music without me if I'm not in the mood or if it's a band that doesn't interest me.

There is one caveat I'll mention, though: The independence of introverts can backfire if you both become so independent that you start running on parallel tracks, spending much of your time pursuing individual interests and fun, and letting togetherness take a backseat. Of course, this can happen in any long-term relationship—you get comfortable, you get busy, you start taking each other for granted. It happens. But it might take introverts longer to notice, since we don't naturally crave a great deal of companionship. Start doing too much separately, and parallel tracks could begin drifting in different directions. That's where introvert fun can become relationship trouble.

"Introverts as couples can flatline," says Nathan Feiles, LCSW, a counselor in New York City who for several years wrote the *Relationships in Balance* blog for the website Psych Central. "It takes a great amount of effort from one or the other. I wouldn't say they have to become an extrovert, but one of them has to step up to bring the other with them, or the relationship will flatline. They will want to stay in all the time, want to shut down."

And it's not always wise—or even preferable—to avoid any and all more-the-merrier events. Sometimes attending parties is fun even for introverts, sometimes it's a gesture of love or solidarity with your party host. Sometimes you need to get out and about for professional reasons.

I enjoy parties now and then, especially those that are neither too big (overwhelming) nor too small (potential performance pressure). Happily, Tom and I feel similarly about parties, so we can go together and usually want to leave around the same time. Sometimes we'll meet midparty, outside or in a quiet room, away from the fuss, to take a breather, regroup, and consult on whether it's time to slip away or if we're game to plunge back in for another round. (We used to step outside for cigarettes, but I finally quit smoking. I think one reason I smoked as long as I did was because smoke breaks are such a great way to step away from the action.)

Like Tom and me, most introvert-introvert couples find ways to support each other through, and eventually out of, extroverted fun. They work up signals, develop code phrases, learn to recognize signs in each other that the fun is coming to an end.

When they've had enough of a social event, Beth and her husband use the phrases "I'm fading" or "I'm wilting," which Beth endorses because you can say them in front of other people without causing offense. "We don't like to make excuses; that just doesn't feel honest. We'd rather just thank our hosts and make a graceful exit."

Among some couples, all it takes is raised eyebrows to signal that the party's over. "We have a system of looks and hand signals we've worked out to get each other out of situations," says Doug M. "To rescue each other from chatterboxes or say 'I'm getting sick of this, wanna go soon?'"

In fact, Doug and his introverted bride even took a break from their own wedding reception. "At a certain point partway through dinner, we both decided that we were sick of being onstage and the center of attention. So we exchanged looks and went back to the catering kitchen and hung out with the caterers for a while. They were focused on their tasks and we had some nice peace and quiet, away from making small talk with extended family."

As an introvert, it's pretty likely that at some point you have been accused of pooping a party. So it's nice to be in a relationship with someone who is happy to be a partner in party pooping, and for whom a party isn't necessary to have fun at all. Finding someone who enjoys quiet pleasures with you is the next best thing (if not even better) to being alone. Equally wonderful is finding someone who can venture out into the noisier world with you, and retreat when necessary.

"We've been to probably hundreds of events over the past fifteen years, between concerts, receptions, donor events, galas, and holiday gatherings," says Beth. "We've learned to enjoy them as much as possible, mostly because we both agree that the best part about going out is coming home!"

Whee! Fun with Extroverts

Keeping Up with the Party People

Generally speaking, we know what extroverts enjoy: People. And more people. And maybe a few more people. They like parties. They like fuss and bother. They like running around. They like lots of things that exhaust introverts if we don't pace ourselves.

If you have paired up with an extrovert, there's probably something you like about riding that person's energy. Some of us really do enjoy being out and about but don't choose to put our energy into making things happen ourselves, or to keep the party going without backup. Nothing wrong with this, and it's even something you can be open about. Who isn't flattered to know that they're good at something, and that they are needed? (To an extent, of course. Needing is good, clinging is not so good.)

Ray-Mel, for example, is a pretty social guy, but he particularly likes being social with his gregarious wife, who does most of the heavy lifting conversation-wise when they're with people they don't know well. And as an artist for whom attending art openings is part of the job, Ray-Mel finds his wife's talent for talk particularly helpful at those. "She's great at networking, given her engaging manner. I'm not that good at it. There are times she's gone places with me because I want her and need her."

To some extent, introverts can become a little dependent on their extroverts to be the mouth of the operation, and not all extroverts love that. Brett, whose fiancée is on the cusp of extroversion, says, "She absolutely adores my introversion, except when we get around a large group of people. She wishes that I, like her, would come out of my shell when in a group setting. We certainly don't fight about it, but her disappointment is made clear."

And Nancy knows that Susan sometimes wishes they had the same attitude toward parties. "One source of our tension is that I go to parties, and before I even walk in the door I'm considering my exit strategy," says Nancy. "She's thinking, *Fun time!*"

But the extroverts we love learn to live with it, and we go and do our best because that's what you do for love. Sometimes you just have to nut up and make the scene, show up, chit the chat, and put on a good face.

"My wife used to work for a big company, so there would be company Christmas parties—introvert hell," says Doug H. "I would go and it would be one engineer and a thousand business-people. But I figured, for four hours I can act like a good husband and go to the party with my wife because it looks good for her."

That's the right attitude. Nevertheless, Doug is not the least bit sorry that his wife now works for a smaller company where the annual holiday party is for employees only.

(These days Doug and his wife's favorite thing to do together is watch their three sons march in the Ohio State marching band—one of the things that brought them together in the first place. Like their dad, all three boys play trombone. "I can't wait to march with all my boys at alumni reunions for the rest of my life," says Doug. Which is so adorable I want to hug them all.)

Besides, even though we may whine and drag our feet, we sometimes find that we enjoy ourselves despite ourselves, that taking a cultural excursion into the extroverted world can be a lot of fun if we go in with an open mind.

Laura's boyfriend has all the earmarks of a raging extrovert. "This is a guy who goes to Burning Man," Laura says—which is saying a lot. Burning Man is an arty, uninhibited, counterculture, proudly weird multiday event in the desert, and the very thought of it makes me want to hide under my desk. But, Laura continues, she did once go with him to a Halloween party in costume (something else that makes me sweat) and ended up having a grand time. "He was a Blue Man and I was the Blue Man groupie. We went to this wild big party in the Venice Beach area, and being able to go and disappear into this crowd of people who were all in their costumes . . . I didn't have to talk to people, the music was loud—it was about watching the scene and being part of that scenery."

Stepping out of your comfort zone can be good for you. It can be healthy, even fun, and it can be good for your relationship, especially if your extrovert truly respects and sympathizes with your introverted ways. And I don't mean sympathizes in a "poor socially awkward introvert" way; I mean in an "I know this is not your favorite thing to do and I know how to make it easier" way.

Kristen's "social bug" husband is glad to have her with him at extrovertish events that require lots of handshaking and meeting and greeting, but he also looks after her. "He knows I don't like to be abandoned in these situations and usually will hang around close by and take me to the next person with him instead of letting me get cornered by a chatterbox," she says. "We've also gotten to a point in our relationship where I can just give him a 'look' and he knows I'm done and it's time to go."

Ah yes, "the look" again. If you don't already have one, it's a good idea to agree on one. You know, that unspoken shorthand that develops between couples. Two raised eyebrows. A twitch of the head doorward. A surreptitious finger-point. Something to subtly say, "It's been fun, now I'm done."

And if it doesn't work and your extrovert is not willing to stop the fun, then what? Bringing two cars is a not-terrible preemptive strike, but this might not go over well with all extroverts. So, in the name of love, you will sometimes just have to accept that you're stuck for a while. Make the best of it and/or hide in the bathroom for a breather. And console yourself with the assurance that you now have a bargaining chip for the next time you want to skip the party or want company for introvertish fun.

Because, of course, fun with extroverts shouldn't be all about doing only extroverted things. You want your extrovert to enjoy doing quiet things with you. Movies, music, travel, and get-togethers with good friends are pretty common ground for introvert and extrovert fun. Sometimes you might adapt your good time a little to accommodate your extrovert. Elizabeth likes hiking more than her girlfriend does, so Elizabeth does her longer hikes with other people and goes for walks on short trails in nearby parks with her girlfriend. "We always have a nice time. She thinks it's cute that I can identify a lot of birds."

And sometimes having an extrovert around can add new dimension even to activities that fall more on the introvert side. When Elizabeth and her girlfriend saw a sculpture at an art museum that they found compelling but didn't understand, they looked awhile, speculated a bit, and then Elizabeth was ready to move on. Her extroverted girlfriend, however, insisted on going to the museum's front desk to ask the woman there about the sculpture. "The woman returned with a binder filled with pictures and descriptions of all the outdoor sculptures," says Elizabeth. "I was ready to walk away and accept the fact that I'd never know the meaning of the sculpture because I don't like to cause waves or draw attention to myself. But my girlfriend was having none of that. She was determined to find the answer, and I really appreciated that about her."

A lot of introverts said that the introverty activity in which their extroverts are often happy—if not relieved—to participate is that TV couch party I described earlier: Stretchy pants, lots of snacks, and TV. All extroverts get plumb wore out sometimes, even if they don't know it or can't admit it. Extroverts in general aren't as experienced as we are in monitoring energy expenditure because they don't have to be. The more they do, the more they do, gaining energy from going full throttle. Until they hit the wall, whether they know it or not. You might be able to tell before they do. The sparkle might go out of their eyes. They might seem to be milling around more than actually doing things. They might just sound reluctant when they respond to invitations. That's when you can show them a thing or two, even if you have to grab their arm and drag them off the dance floor (metaphorically or not).

"Come weekends, if she needs to sit in front of the TV in her pajamas and eat popcorn, she needs someone to say, 'Oh, honey, it's OK,'" says Nancy about her busy, busy wife. "I think for her mental health she really does need that, and she needs someone to give her permission."

Nancy also knows that while her wife frequently bubbles over with ideas of things they can do, places they can go, and people they can see, if Nancy is just agreeable and patient, many of these exhausting ideas eventually blow over. "Part of the fun for her is thinking about doing them," she says. Actually getting out and doing them is optional, which is fine by Nancy.

But, of course, for activities or events that you just can't agree on, there is always the "you go ahead, I'll have a quiet evening at home" form of introvert-extrovert fun time. Couples that are comfortable uncoupling for periods of time to pursue separate interests can stave off all kinds of unnecessary resentment. Your job, as the introvert, is to assure your extrovert that you are OK with staying in, and you are OK with your extrovert going out without you. And you have to mean it. No pained sighs, muttered asides, or gentle whimpers. No texting every ten minutes. No attitudes of suffering forbearance. I'm not saying you would do those things, but just in case you think you might, I'm saying you shouldn't. If it's hard to let your extrovert go out and have fun without you, you might not be cut out for a mixed relationship. You might be happier with a fellow introvert.

And, of course, that goes for the extrovert, too. If you get attitude about going separate ways sometimes or if you find you have to have introvert-friendly fun on your own more often than not, then it's time for some heart-to-hearts. Because if you can't share fun with the one you love, you might be on the road to resentment. And that's really no fun.

When Enough Is Too Much

People Versus Isolation for Introvert Couples

Do you get enough socializing in your life? Do you get too much? Do you and your partner share the same social needs?

When I asked Ed if he and his equally introverted wife ever find themselves getting isolated, he was baffled. "I don't understand the question," he said. "We're as social as we choose to be. We have friends and family we could visit if we would like, but we rarely want to."

Ed and Rebecca are introverts in equilibrium.

Whereas although both Arden and her husband are introverts, she needs more socializing than he does. He's agreed to a couple of outings a month; otherwise, she goes out with friends. She also sometimes arranges dinner parties and small get-togethers with their friends, and her husband enjoys those despite himself. This is a workable compromise for them.

Anne has resigned herself to her introverted husband's

discomfort with holidays with her family, "because he has to make nice to fifteen people," she says. This was a point of contention until Anne gave up her expectations and decided to enjoy her family sans husband. "I've decided I'm going to adopt a 'when in Rome' attitude," she says. Anne is making the best of it—a good plan under such circumstances, as long as you can do it without building up resentment.

When introverts find each other, they can lose track of everyone else. Sometimes that's fine, sometimes lack of other interaction becomes too much for one person, sometimes two introverts can enable unhealthy isolation in each other.

In a way, if one person in a couple is more introverted than the other, the need to negotiate socializing resembles what an introvert-extrovert couple must do: give-and-take, and maybe some ground rules.

Early in our relationship, my somewhat-less-introverted-than-me husband and I agreed that neither of us was required to attend any event with the other, unless by special request. We make no assumptions about each other's participation in anything, but we also are allowed to say, "This one matters," when we really do want the other's presence.

And nowadays, because I work at home and have lots of solitude and he has a business that requires lots of interaction, we are working out how to make sure he doesn't burn out on people and I don't go all Jack Nicholson "redrum" from isolation. This is still a work in progress, but I try to make plans with friends as often as I can and we try to get out of the house and do something every weekend.

In some ways, the understanding introverts share makes social life a lot easier. Introverts understand that staying home alone is not odd. It's acceptable, even necessary, and so when the need arises for one reason or another, nobody has to feel guilty. And Tom and I are good at making excuses for each other when one of us turns up at an event without the other. Actually, at this point our friends are pretty used to seeing us out and about uncoupled. They know how we are.

And introverts know exactly how it feels when socializing just isn't feeling great. "She understands what's going through my mind when I'm at a party and feeling out of place and uncomfortable," says Doug M. And, he says, "She, like I, recoils at the thought of going to a party where we don't know anyone."

Another introvert will duck into a quiet spot with you midparty to assess whether you're both still having fun, and understands if you cry uncle early in the evening. Another introvert knows what it means to have hit your threshold.

Julie tells a story about having friends come by to see their new apartment, which turned into four people spending the night, breakfast the next day, and hours more hanging out, until she and her introverted boyfriend were giving each other panicky eyes, wondering if their friends would ever leave. Finally, *finally*, the friends all trooped off to see a movie. "As soon as they all left, we both just collapsed on the couch," says Julie. "My boyfriend said something like 'How do people do that? Just hang out with each other constantly?' After that we both just went about our ways in silence for most of the rest of the day."

Ah yes. An introvert understands that it's possible to just plain run out of words, and when that happens, silence is golden, necessary, and a honkin' big relief. My work often requires me to travel with groups of people for days at a time and Tom knows to give me wide berth when I come home from one of those trips, to allow me recovery time. And after we take a togetherness-heavy vacation, I've noticed that Tom needs to retreat to his cave for a while. Hard to imagine that anyone could ever get enough of me, but apparently it's possible. The first time I noticed this, I got my feelings hurt. But after thinking it through, I got it. Togetherness is wonderful—until you've had enough.

There are some drawbacks in introvert-introvert relationships, however—you might both have an urge to socialize, but not the skill. "It will usually be my idea to go to parties or other gatherings, but then we are both terrible at socializing so we just end up in the corner together," says Julie. If that happens more often than not, maybe it's time to start initiating your own get-togethers, so that you'll know everyone there and will be in your own comfort zone.

While we nurture each other's introverted ways, though, we have to also keep in mind that introversion can be overindulged. Too much solitude can become isolation and the beginning of a downward spiral. For introverts, solitude is good for deep thinking, but thinking can slip into rumination, and rumination is proven to lead to depression. Or, at the very least, crabbiness. "We noticed very early on in our relationship that if we went too long without socializing, we'd start getting snippy with each other over little things," Beth says. "We can completely enable each other to just stay in and not do anything or see anyone."

And so sometimes you have to drag each other out. Beth and her husband have come up with a fun way to keep isolation in check: They "kidnap" each other. "The 'kidnapper' is in charge of choosing an activity and making it happen, while the other person is left in the dark," says Beth. "When we approach an activity this way, we're infinitely less likely to talk ourselves out of it."

There's another risk to overindulging introversion, and that's the possibility of letting your wider support network drift away. When everything is going well, you might not notice. But life is complicated. It's unpredictable. Things happen and you never know when you might need backup. Don't let too much time pass between contact with people you care about. If they care about you, they will respect your need for space, so if you don't make an effort, you might start drifting apart, and it might feel awkward to reach out when you really need a friend. All people need people. Even introverts. Within reason, of course.

When Two's Company, Three's a Headache, and Four Makes Me Hide in the Bathroom

Coping with Your Extrovert's Need for People

People who need people. Lots and lots of people. We call them extroverts and we love them. Their easy connection with other human beings is often admirable, and often even useful. But sometimes . . . just sometimes . . .

"I'm an introvert and my husband is an extrovert," a woman commented on my blog. "Our latest compromise is that he agreed to no longer roll down my passenger-side window in the car and engage in small talk as we pass neighbors on the street. It sounds a little crazy, I know, but it was really making me insane. On extreme extrovert days, my partner seemed to go out of his way, traveling random side streets, looking for people to say hi to while I just wanted to get to the grocery store (or wherever)."

"She's one of those people who will get into lengthy conversations with shop clerks just to have interaction," Nancy says. "Sometimes it's fine, sometimes I'm thinking 'tick-tock, tick-tock.'"

And Kristen's extroverted husband "talks constantly to almost everyone and anyone," she says. "Sometimes I feel embarrassed—like, can we just go to the store and buy one item without you making a bunch of noise?"

Not that we never appreciate extroverts' skills. Sometimes they're exactly what we need. Tyler's sociable wife made their transition a lot easier when his job took them to a new town where they knew no one. And Tyler says that his default is to stay home, which isn't always good for him. "That can spiral out of control, down a dark path," he says. His extroverted wife helps keep him off that dark path by making plans for them both, to be sure he gets out of the house and among people.

Nancy, too, finds her wife's more-the-merrier ways help ensure that she doesn't get isolated. "I really depend on her so much for my social life," she says. "*So* much. She'll invite people a hundred times more to my one, and I'm glad she does, because indulging in my introversion to the nth degree is not healthy for me."

So having an extrovert in your life to keep you connected with the world outside your head can be a good thing if you find that too much solitude takes you places you'd rather not be.

There are other introverts, however, who socialize more as a loving gesture than because they want or need to. Brett's fiancée loves getting together with people a lot more than Brett does.

"I could go my entire life without socializing," Brett says. "There is nothing about socializing that pleases me. It's not torture or anything, but it doesn't make me happy. I'm indifferent. If I'm going to spend time around a group of people, it needs to have a purpose. Getting together to get together seems like a waste of time." While his fiancée has become more of a homebody since they've met, she still loves getting together with friends. Brett will join her if she asks, which she sometimes does even though she knows he'd rather not.

The trick for mixed couples is finding the balance, where the introvert isn't perpetually exhausted and the extrovert doesn't feel trapped at home, or resentful about never having a date for social events. Because even when we understand and respect each other's needs in the abstract, real-world balance can be tricky, requiring give-and-take, trial and error, flexibility, self-awareness, and occasional sacrifice on the part of both.

Maybe balance means you set a general rule of one night out, one night in on weekends. Or weeknights in, weekends out. Maybe you agree to throw parties, but limit the number of guests. Maybe this circle of friends you can handle, but that circle of friends just wears you out. Susan has one friend in particular who is just plain too much for Nancy. "Susan will say, 'I'll just go have coffee with her,' and I say fine," says Nancy. "Susan has really taken care of that friendship, but there also have been times where she has said, 'OK, this is a command performance,' and I get it."

Remember (and remind your extrovert) that it's much easier for you to say yes to socializing if you can also sometimes say no without negative repercussions, and it's much easier for you to show up if you know you can leave when you've had enough.

Times when your extrovert is antsy and you're feeling introvertish, you might be able to come up with outings that satisfy you both. For introverts, small groups can be easier than large groups, though big crowds—such as sporting events or street fairs—can be easiest of all if we are not required to talk to anyone. Getting together with close friends is much easier than meeting new people, and dinner parties with friends can be very pleasant.

You might find that the sooner you know about a big event, the better. Lots of lead time allows us to gear up and gird ourselves. It also helps with that ever-important energy management, allowing us to schedule our lives so that we can store up energy before a draining event, and have recovery time after.

Of course, with long lead time we sometimes run into the problem of finding that when the planned event rolls around, we regret agreeing to go in the first place. Such is life. Sometimes when that happens, you simply have to nut up and make the best of it. If you've been keeping pace with your extrovert for a while, generously and without griping, however, you might have stored up enough goodwill and Brownie points to say, "I know we planned this, but I'm really not feeling it. Would you hate it if I bail?"

You might even be able to talk your extrovert into bailing with you. Tyler has talked his wife into slowing down sometimes, pointing out when her schedule is getting frenetic. "I like to think I've helped her find balance in her own life, too," he says. "I almost think that her default is to say yes to these situations and yes to friends, and the idea of staying home to be with herself is kind of foreign."

Extroverts need quiet time, too, and time alone with their special someone. It's just that they sometimes need you to remind them.

Saved by the Extrovert!

How Your Extrovert
Can Help You Through Social Events

Extroverts' social skills and high socializing thresholds might be exhausting at times, but they also can come in very handy. Bless the extroverts who understand introversion enough to save us when we are starting to crumble. The ones who glibly come up with alibis when you need to leave an event early, the ones who start saying their farewells when they see "the look" that says it's time for the fun to end, the ones who say, "Don't worry, I'll handle this one, you can stay home." The ones who run interference for us with people who don't get it.

This is the sort of thing sensitive extroverts start picking up on early in the relationship, and the closer the relationship gets, the better they get at it. You might as well put them to work for you by talking about your fears, tensions, and dislikes, letting them know your thresholds, and then deciding together how to deal with it. You can then hope they'll be OK with putting their people skills to work by running interference for you, which will ensure that everyone has enough—and not too much—fun.

For example, before her company picnic, Elizabeth's girlfriend went so far as to brief her boss on Elizabeth's introverted ways. "She told her boss that she shouldn't be concerned that I'm quiet, and that I'm having a good time even if it doesn't appear that way," Elizabeth says. "I felt totally comfortable sitting in my lawn chair in the midst of all her coworkers and I didn't feel like I had to make idle chitchat. I actually had a very nice time."

Tyler's wife has run interference for him with her family, which celebrates birthdays with much hoopla. "Everybody goes to somebody's house and there's, like, twenty people," Tyler says. "It seriously gives me anxiety to even think about that. So she went to her parents and said that for my birthday, it's just us and that's it. She understood and kind of cleared the way."

A sensitive extrovert might also notice and help out when you're running out of steam in a social situation.

"Jaime can always tell when I've had enough," says Brett. "When I'm happy and having a good time, she says my eyes glow and sparkle. When I'm done, they shut off. Grow cold. That's when she knows I've checked out."

If you talk this kind of thing through, your extrovert should be OK when you have to wander off, physically or mentally, when you've hit your wall, and perhaps even pick up conversational slack so others don't notice.

Some extroverts will figure this kind of stuff out by themselves. Others might need a little nudge to see it your way, which means it will be up to you to let them know what events stress you out. "I love your family, but too many of them at once is overwhelming. Can we do them just a couple at a time?" Or "I'll go to your company party with you if you promise that when I let you know I've hit the wall, we can leave." Or "I don't mind going to these get-togethers with you if you don't mind that sometimes I'll have to mentally check out a little, or wander away for a breather."

Your extrovert might even come up with sensitive ways to explain you to other people: "She's fine, she just needs to clear her head now and then. It's an introvert thing." (Happily, more and more people these days are learning about introversion and will understand what "an introvert thing" means.)

And if you're seriously shutting down, the thoughtful extrovert will start wrapping up the fun without being grumpy about it. With all their people skills, extroverts can be quite good at extricating themselves (and you) when they think the party is over. When they have company and the evening seems to be dragging on, Nancy lets Susan lead the guests to the door because she can do it "without any tension in her voice," Nancy says. This sort of thing isn't always easy for us introverts, who may be too tapped out to be diplomatic, or may carry residual feelings of shame for our introverted nature—it feels so unkind to tell people you've had enough when they might already (mistakenly) suspect you don't like people.

One of the most trying situations an introvert can be in is having, or being, a houseguest. Nancy and Susan have lots of family, ergo lots of multiday visits, although they have established a three-

day maximum on most. Despite the dread with which she antici-
pates family visits, Nancy usually ends up enjoying herself. "And
I'm happy to have them come back," she says. "Just not tomorrow."
And Susan is sensitive to Nancy's frazzle point. "She's gotten very
protective of me, particularly with lengthy family stays where we're
all sort of living on top of each other," Nancy says. "She'll say, 'I'll
just tell them you're taking a nap,' or 'Go on, go run the errands.
I know you want to be by yourself.'"

When we visit his family, my husband always brings me coffee
in bed so I am well fortified before the morning chitchat. And when
he sees me reaching my frazzle point, he'll shoo me out of the house
to take a walk. Exercise as escapism.

A little communication, a little negotiation, a few schemes and
strategies, and you might find your extrovert can take a lot of pressure off you when you need it. A generous extrovert can come in
very handy.

The Greatness of Escape

Getting Time Alone

Sometimes, no matter how much you love the other person, you just want to be alone. Really, truly alone.

I know couples who in decades of marriage have not spent more than a couple of nights apart, and those only by necessity. Different strokes and all that, but I sure don't get it. I love my husband but sometimes the only way I can really, truly feel like me is when I'm alone. Completely and utterly alone.

For me, that means actually packing a bag and taking a trip by myself.

I don't belong to the cult of busy people and my life isn't terribly demanding, but occasionally, any other person's needs feel like too much. My patterns of living are different from my husband's. He's an early bird, I'm a night owl. He requires a square meal every night, I am satisfied to graze. He likes the company of the television or music nearly all the time, I like silence. Nothing wrong with his habits, they're just different. And sometimes I need to be purely me.

And those are some of the reasons I love traveling alone.

I've taken several writing retreats to manage book deadlines, renting a small place with a kitchen in a pretty location where I slip into a somewhat haphazard routine of writing, eating, hiking, writing, exercising, staring into space, writing, reading. Maybe I'll stream a movie or TV show on my computer until I drift off to sleep. Sometimes I just drift off to sleep. Going days without conversation doesn't bother me in the least.

Tom is never terribly thrilled by this—he would prefer having me at home. Still, as an introvert himself, after a day or two alone at home, he also slips into his own rhythm and finds he enjoys the solitude, too.

Being alone with someone you love is great. But sometimes the need to be alone with only yourself is necessary to keeping well calibrated.

Afiq says that even with a young woman he liked very much, he found himself feeling suffocated by togetherness. "I just don't like the idea that as a couple we have to hang out all the time 'cause I really need my time alone after we hang out a lot!" he says.

"I see 'alone time' as time with just myself and my books or computer. She sees 'alone time' as just the two of us," says Brett. "It's adorable and flattering, to be honest. I love how much she wants to spend time together. About ninety-nine percent of the time, I'm right there with her. During that one percent, though, I need to be alone."

Rather than make a case over this, Brett ekes out solitude as he can. Sometimes he'll go home for lunch instead of meeting his fiancée as usual. "That's a solid hour, at least, when it's just me and my thoughts," he says. If he can't do that, he might leave work a little early, to get home before she does. He's even resorted to a little harmless subterfuge, skipping a night class once to just spend some time with himself. (This is not a good idea if there are any trust issues between you and your partner; in that case, transparency is advisable.)

Sometimes you have to savor the moments of solitude that arise naturally. Tone gets her solitude after Tony has gone to work, and it's her favorite time of day. "I walk downstairs to make myself a cup of coffee and spend an hour or three just waking up slowly and starting the day."

When we first moved in together, Tom worked at home and I had an office job. He was there when I woke up in the morning, there when I got home in the evening. As much as I loved him, I finally had to ask him to please make plans one night a week so I could get some home-alone time. Which he did.

Actually, this was before what I call the Great Bedtime Epiphany, when I realized that just because we were a couple, I was not compelled to go to bed at the same time as he. Wow, what a forehead slapper that was. It's not like we were getting into bed for marital antics. He would go to sleep, I would lie awake and stare at the ceiling. Or else I would read awhile and drift off, only to find myself wide awake an hour or two later because I wasn't respecting my natural sleep rhythms. Nowadays, many nights I stay up long after Tom is asleep in bed, reading, watching TV, messing around online. Happily alone.

Not getting enough time alone can cause tension in a relationship in and of itself, whether or not you immediately realize where your sudden snippiness or resentment is coming from. Sometimes all it takes is an evening, a Saturday, even a few hours of solitude to recalibrate. Having a room of your own can help, especially if you feel comfortable closing the door. (I find that difficult to do when my husband is in the house; it feels not nice.)

Even though I do get enough snippets of solitude, sometimes I need something hard-core. That's when I pack a bag for a solo jaunt. And I'm not the only introvert who is happy to travel solo.

"Personal travel has always been alone," says Shannon. "I usually look forward to at least one flight somewhere a year, and a week to two-week road trip, just me and my dog with no commitment, no obligations, and usually not much of a plan. I've only taken a vacation with a girlfriend once, to Vegas, and it was fun, but by the end of four days, I needed a vacation from the vacation!"

"I love, love, love traveling alone, especially when I can drive to the destination rather than fly," says Elizabeth. "I really enjoy long road trips, absent any time constraints. I generally don't listen to music while I drive; I prefer the hum of the tires."

"Last August I drove to far West Texas for a vacation by myself," says Drew. "Although I'm sure I would have enjoyed the trip with someone else, I wanted to go by myself. I just felt compelled to do it alone. I took it all in without distraction. On my hikes in the mountains, I never encountered another person, only the deer, javelinas, and a mountain lion that was thankfully more afraid of me than I was of it. I love the feeling of being entirely alone in nature, with no one around for miles."

I share that sentiment.

So this is one of the compromises in my marriage. While Tom is OK with my solo travel, he won't ever feel the same joyous anticipation I do. Who can blame him for that? But he understands that without solo adventures, I get restless; a dark cloud, weighted with resentment, settles on our marriage. My solo trips are good for me, and so they're good for us. And he knows I always come home.

If you are drawn to the idea of traveling alone but your partner is uncomfortable with it, try setting some ground rules. Daily check-ins, perhaps, or frequent text check-ins. Set limits on the duration of trips. Plan a couples trip (or two) for every solo trip. If you have kids, maybe give them a few days with Grandma and Grandpa so your partner isn't parenting solo. Tom and I have occasionally even boarded the dog when I travel alone so he doesn't have to rush home from work every day to cater to canine needs.

I hope that by the time you are spending a lot of time together you will have reached a point where you can freely express your need for solitude sometimes. But keep in mind that your partner might find it frightening or threatening and you may have to visit the topic more than once before you are both comfortable. You'll want to explain that your need for solitude has nothing to do with anyone but yourself. That you are not trying to get away from your partner; it's about your need to be alone with yourself. Explain that without alone time, your mood goes sour and you're no fun. Explain that it is good for the relationship.

I like Drew's description of the "pinging" that goes on when someone else is around—even if you're not interacting, there's that little part of your brain that remains aware of the other person. For some introverts, those pings can be a racket that interferes with our thoughts.

Try promising some special time together when your alone time is over. Be open about what you will be doing and where you will go. Choose activities that your partner wouldn't enjoy anyway. Perhaps even make a routine of it; every Tuesday is fend-for-yourself night, or each of you is entitled to a certain number of weekends every year to do with as you please.

An extrovert in particular might need lots of reassurance before he or she is comfortable with your need for alone time. But if you need it, as many of us do, you owe it to both of you to get it—whether for an evening, a weekend, or more.

Maybe If I Ignore It,
It Will Go Away

Introverts and Conflict

Kristen's first husband was as introverted as she. "We initially connected because we understood each other's introverted nature, which seemed really rare to me back then," she says. "It ultimately failed, however, because neither one of us ever wanted to rock the boat. Serious issues were swept under the rug, and ultimately it just imploded because we weren't communicating well and drifted into separate worlds."

Yep. Suppressed conflict is one of the big risks introverted couples face. When I asked introverts how they handle conflict, quite a few said, "Badly," or "I try to avoid it," or "I physically leave the room."

"He tends to shut down and withdraw when things are bothering him. I'll finally have to pull it out of him. It's the classic fight-or-flight response. I fight, he flights," says Arden.

"I handle conflict by usually backing down and letting one side win in order to stop it from continuing," says Nick S., a 24-year-old grad student. "I try to avoid conflict even if I feel strongly about one side over the other."

"Nick really won't confront me about anything and he just gets really stressed and apologetic if I bring up something that makes me unhappy," his girlfriend, Julie, confirms. "I don't think we fight very often, but I will usually get pretty emotional, then calm down, then we usually just talk about it and come to some kind of resolution or apology. He stays pretty unemotional and doesn't yell."

Sometimes it's hard to tell if you've handled conflict or just deflected it. And sometimes trying not to have conflict causes more trouble than it avoids because feelings are just not very amenable to being stuffed. Sooner or later, they come out, whether you want them to or not.

"I'll get upset about stuff that's been going on for a while and I won't bring it up at first," says Julie. "I just feel like I shouldn't bring it up right away, that I'm probably overreacting. Then if I get upset about something else, if I've had a bad day, it just all comes spilling out."

Ouch. I can relate to that. I'm a silent seether. When something upsets me, it can take a long time for me to process it, to decide if it's legitimate, if it's worth bringing up, if I can trust my own feelings about it. I turn it over and over in my head, looking at it this way and that way, considering all the possible ways to interpret my husband's actions and my anger, how conversation about whatever it is might unfold, what I might say, what he might say, round and round and round in my head. And all that time, I'm fully aware of

Tom's furtive, worried looks as he wonders what fresh hell will burst from me when I finally get around to saying whatever I need to say.

This is not fair to him and, worse, by the time I let it out, so much pressure has built up that my emotions explode like popcorn in hot oil. By then, even a small irritation has become overblown in my mind, and what could have been easily handled turns into a big friggin' problem.

Not good at all.

Too bad not liking to deal with conflict is not the same thing as not having conflict. Conflict is inevitable in any relationship, and how couples handle it is the best indicator of the health of their relationship. But while extroverts are likely to want to process emotions by talking them out (more on that in the next chapter), introverts tend to process internally, so we might keep complaints to ourselves and just stew in our own juices, which can lead to "'silent suffering' and a marriage without true intimacy," says therapist Carol Lennox.

To avoid all that silent suffering, introverted couples have to learn to speak up when they have something that needs saying, and learn to listen without retreating when something needs hearing. (An important aside: Introversion and extroversion play only a small part in our conflict-management skills. Like so much else in our lives, this, too, can be traced back to the family we grew up in. That's where we learned to deal—or not deal—with conflict and negative feelings.)

Still, a lot of introverts know that for them, retreat before discussion is necessary for a problem to be peaceably worked out.

"Habitually, I withdraw—or prefer to—until my temper cools," says Melissa. "My intense emotions usually blow over in a day or two."

"I think we both have a tendency to avoid problems and don't always talk about them right away," says Gary. "My wife likes to talk things through, but she finds it difficult to bring matters up. I think about matters long and hard sometimes before I can articulate what I want to say. And I prefer getting it out without what I experience as interruption, and I think she, and others, experience as dialogue."

For this reason Gary likes to express difficult emotions in an email. Me, too. And Gary's wife and my husband feel the same way about this: They hate it. "That in itself has become an issue," says Gary. Indeed. My husband laid down the law on that pretty early in our relationship (way back when it was letters, not emails). His rule is: Talking not writing.

I'm a writer by temperament and trade so I feel a little hobbled by this, but I mostly try to comply. I've even, on occasion, written down what I've needed to say and read it to him. But I understand why this might be unpleasant and intimidating: Writing things down allows us to construct what seems like a neat, airtight, unemotional package. Bringing things up face to face in a timely manner, before I have stewed them into a red-hot mess, allows a discussion to develop from heartfelt emotion, tremulous voice and all, rather than chilly analysis.

Not that this is easy, mind you. It's been a steep learning curve for me, and Tom is having to learn not to get heated even if it's a tough discussion, since this will shut me down and get us nowhere. But we're trying.

Now, if you happen to be a joker, that can be a good thing. Marriage expert John Gottman has positive things to say about couples who can break the tension with a little joke when they're fighting. Like Doug M. and his wife. "We have similar and skewed outlooks on life, our default tone for most things is to joke about them," he says. "But there are times when you apparently have to be serious in life. We are very open with each other, on the same wavelength."

Naturally you don't want to joke so much that it derails real discussion, but a little shared laugh mid-squabble reconnects you to each other and to positive feelings when you might otherwise be awash in negativity.

And the good news is that dealing with conflict can be learned— either through trial and error or with professional help. Ed and Rebecca did the former, even though Ed is a yeller and Rebecca is not. "I tend to shrink from it and clam up," she says. But she now understands that the yelling eventually turns to discussion that will lead to the source of the problem. "We find middle ground, or agree to disagree when there is none," says Ed. "We don't part ways—to sleep, school, work, or even to run an errand, angry."

In individual counseling, Gary learned strategies to stay present in conflict rather than fleeing it. "I literally 'ground' myself, putting both feet flat on the floor and without my legs crossed. I intentionally sit up straighter than I often do, and I maintain an open posture with my arms and hands either at my sides or on my knees, seeking to express I'm open to what she wants to say. And when I start to feel anxious, I work at staying present instead of leaving/ avoiding the conversation and going off to a room by myself."

Beth credits therapy in both her and her husband's histories for their effective conflict-management strategies. "We're pretty tuned in to the other person's mood and can tell just by how we say hello on the phone if something's up. We've learned not to continue to be mad once it's clear the other person knows what there is to be mad about, by taking responsibility or acknowledging the problem. That helps to de-escalate things quickly. We've also had to practice knowing when we have the bandwidth to talk about something difficult. If one or both of us doesn't have the energy to deal with a confrontation, we can usually negotiate talking about it later or dialing down the intensity."

Nobody—introvert or extrovert—really enjoys conflict, but it's not something that can be avoided in a healthy relationship. Because problems are like splinters: If you don't extricate them, they get infected, and what started as a small problem can well turn into something ugly and twice as painful.

Hey, You, Get Outta My Face

When Introverts and Extroverts Collide

Again: No matter how much you love each other (or maybe even especially because you love each other and the stakes are high), sometimes you are going to disagree, butt heads, need to clear the air. It's necessary, important, and no fun at all. (Except the making-up part, of course.) And it can be extra tough when one half of a couple likes to let it all hang out and the other half prefers to hold it all in.

Conflict in introvert-extrovert couples has its own particular challenges—and benefits. The challenges are that extroverts might get right up in your face when there's a problem. The benefits are that extroverts might get right up in your face when there's a problem.

"I tend to shut down and withdraw when I'm upset about something," says Kristen, newly wed to an extreme extrovert. "My instinct is to look for an escape rather than deal with whatever the problem is, or react in a very passive-aggressive way. My husband is the total opposite of this, so he will usually not leave me alone if he senses something is wrong. That's actually a really good thing, even though sometimes he has to pull me out of my silent, angry corner. This is the most healthy, honest, open, and functional relationship I've ever had."

Kristen is not alone in her tendency to shut down. Nancy says she does the same thing but rather than hound her, her wife has learned to give her space before pressing for discussion. "We had one of those little silent treatments recently," Nancy told me. "She said something that was really upsetting to me, and it's almost like it puts a lock on my mouth. I said something and walked out of the room, and she knows by now that she had better give me some space because I'm overwhelmed and I'll say bad things. For me to have a productive conversation, I have to calm down."

After about an hour, the two had a good conversation that would not have been possible if Susan had forced the subject.

"The most recurring theme in my squabbles with my fiancée is my tendency to retreat inward when I know she's upset with me," says Brett. "When I know she's mad or even the slightest bit upset with me, I shut down. I get quiet and find solace in my own mind. She wants to talk it out and resolve issues, but my automatic response is to curl up in my own comfortable emotional space and say very little. I know it's not productive, as it only serves to worsen the argument. However, it seems as if my introversion kicks in immediately, and I'd rather just get comfy in my own head and ride out the storm. I'm not proud of it, but there are times it seems as if I can't control that initial response."

This kind of thing is not unusual, says therapist Nathan Feiles. Extroverts tend to want to get everything out there on the table right away, and their unbridled emotion can overwhelm an introvert. "There may be a more wordy approach to it, a more emotional component," he says. "The introvert tends to be more rational and reasonable about it, less comfortable experiencing the emotion and the ambiguity of it.

"That can be very hard for the extrovert," he continues. "The extrovert often needs to be emotional and needs to be heard and be validated in their emotions." Meanwhile, the introvert is trying to explain it all so that the extrovert will just understand and stop with all the overwhelming emoting.

This tends not to go well.

"When it comes to conflict, I'm always looking for ways to get around it," David says. "For me, getting annoyed with each other is counterproductive. There was a time she would say, 'You're just being Buddhist now.'

"I can be accused of talking too much around things— 'philosophizing' is the word that's used, not getting to the point," he continues. His extroverted wife, however, is more likely to plunge on in, in an angry voice if that's how she's feeling. "Her confrontational style wasn't easy to adjust to," David says. "Maybe I even struggle with it now. Maybe it stings me a bit now. But I know we need to do it."

You do need to do it because trying to avoid conflict is one thing, but if you've gone from trying to sidestep it to just plain shutting down and refusing to engage in it, you may be saddling up one of the most dangerous of the Four Horsemen that marriage expert John Gottman identifies as relationship killers: Stonewalling. Once you start refusing to engage in conflict communication, your relationship is heading into serious trouble.

Introverts' efforts to keep conflict cerebral is of course not because they lack emotions about it. They have plenty of emotions. Oodles of emotions. Whole brains and hearts crammed full of emotions that can get bottled up because we get overwhelmed, or because we're used to keeping ourselves to ourselves.

Doug H.'s wife had to teach him about conflict. "Early on, she would point out when something wasn't right," he says. "She'd had boyfriends before, so she knew what conflict looked like. She taught me how to have a discussion about things I didn't want to talk about."

Like Nancy, however, Doug was not good at responding immediately. Early in their marriage, instead of taking in what his wife said and thinking it through, he just got angry. "I would yell about how I want details and I want them to know exactly how I feel." Doug and his wife figured out that the best way to handle any difficult discussions was for her to let him know there was a problem, let him think about it, and then talk about it.

Naturally, a lot of introvert-extrovert conflicts have nothing to do with introversion and extroversion. (For example, in Kristen's marriage, cheese is an issue. "Whenever he buys cheese, I always eat it all. I don't know why, but I just love cheese and apparently don't think clearly when it comes to cheese.") But if recurring arguments seem to have a subtext, you might explore the possibility that an introversion/extroversion issue is exacerbating a problem. And remember that matters like these—like any intimacy issues—can go all the way back to our childhoods and the ways our brains got wired by our earliest relationships.

If, for example, you had a parent who didn't respect your introversion and was constantly urging you to be different, you might be drawn to extroverts who do the same thing, says therapist Carol Lennox. It's kind of a natural for us to land in relationships that feel familiar, she says, but you might then realize that some of the familiarity is no more pleasant now than it was when you were a kid who just wanted to sit quietly and read. You might be used to having someone urging you to get out and mingle, but that doesn't mean you like it any more as an adult. "I've definitely seen the introvert feel that the extrovert is intruding on their space," Carol says. "And the extrovert feels rejected."

An introvert who feels intruded upon might start withdrawing further in self-protection, and an extrovert who feels rejected might start spending more time away from home with friends or other family. Things can spiral down from there.

Another theory about how we choose our relationships is the "shadow" theory—that we choose partners who contain qualities we wish we had ourselves—our shadow selves.

Introverts who admire extroverts for their extroversion might be attracted to, and attractive to, extroverts, Carol says. But after a while, envy and resentment might slip in. You might become envious of your extrovert's ease with people; your extrovert might start pushing you to stop living vicariously and get out and get extroverted yourself.

If you really do want to be more extroverted, then that's great; your extrovert can provide pointers and encouragement. But if you are really pretty satisfied being the introvert that you are, that "encouragement" might just feel like pressure. And all this goes for the extrovert, too. Maybe your extrovert subconsciously chose you for your calming influence but after a while starts feeling antsy and pinned down.

None of this is fatal to a relationship, though, if you become aware of it and make communication across the divide a priority. This might take a little soul-searching and some tough love—with yourself. What is your contribution to the communication problems? Are you a silent seether? Take my word for it, that doesn't help anything. Try forcing yourself to bring things up before you've ruminated them into a huge issue.

If you find yourself shutting down in conflict, remind yourself that nothing gets solved that way. If you find it hard to compete with your extrovert's flood of words, bring that up at some point when you are both calm. (Bringing it up in the heat of an argument could derail the discussion at hand.) While it's OK to step away and think, if that's what you need, it's only fair to let your partner know that's what you're doing, so he or she doesn't think you're stonewalling. And then it's particularly good form to be the one who brings the topic up again when you're ready to continue the discussion.

"You just have to swallow hard and step outside of your

emotions," says Nancy, who has been with Susan for twenty-three years. "When we do need to talk, we put a premium on productive conversation, and we've worked really, really hard over the years to listen to each other. It's hard to talk productively. It's easy to take potshots at each other. It's also hard to call people on those potshots lovingly rather than hurling another potshot back."

Once you start shooting pots at each other, you risk taking your relationship on a ride on the other three of Gottman's Four Horsemen: Contempt, criticism, and defensiveness. If your conflicts turn into name-calling, put-downs, denials, and finally stonewalling when it all gets too unpleasant, then your relationship could be riding the Four Horsemen into the sunset.

One thing you can do if you find your relationship stuck in repeating struggles is the introvert thing: Read. Gottman's books can be eye-openers when it comes to learning about conflict, and Doug and his wife found Willard F. Harley Jr.'s book, *His Needs, Her Needs: Building an Affair-Proof Marriage*, to be helpful. Books by Harville Hendrix have helped many couples over the years, as has the book *The Five Love Languages* by Gary Chapman.

But if you're struggling and can't seem to pull it together yourselves, a counselor can help you sort through the unspoken issues. Nathan has helped many couples in trouble rewire their faulty communication channels. "When there's middle ground and they're both able to listen to each other and both able to speak for themselves without trying to step over the boundaries into the other person's area, it ends up increasing the connection and communication," he says. "And it's a beautiful thing."

It Must Be Love

Introverts on That Special Feeling

Is this "it"? Is this where happily meets ever after?

Introverts aren't really comfortable with grand love gestures—skywriting at the baseball game, an elaborate public proposal at a restaurant. (Smacks terrifyingly close to having a whole restaurant full of people sing "Happy Birthday to You." Shudder.) You're not likely to meet an introverted Bridezilla—being the center of attention just isn't that important to us. The things that make us feel loved and special aren't big and flashy; they just have to hit the note that gives us a warm tingle.

Introverts can be a little opaque sometimes; we don't wear our emotions on our sleeves. Tone and Tony had a hard time figuring out how the other felt until they had an explicit conversation (and then it was full speed ahead). We also tend to be pretty self-sufficient, which we can take too far sometimes, becoming almost ascetic in our independence. But everyone needs to feel loved, and we all feel love in different ways. Are you getting the kind of love you crave? Have you ever really thought about what makes you feel loved?

Gary Chapman covered this topic in depth in his book *The Five Love Languages: The Secret to Love That Lasts*, a very useful book for couples who feel that their expressions of love aren't being heard. Because the expression of love is a language, we all speak it differently.

I asked introverts what makes them feel loved. Maybe something here will strike a chord with you, or get you thinking about what love feels like when it whispers in your ear.

Anne knew she was onto something good when her new boyfriend made his intentions explicit. "One week we were driving to church and he said, 'Just to be clear, we're in this relationship to see if it would work out toward marriage.' I said, 'Thank you for clarifying.' I thought it was very responsible of him, very manly of him."

Rebecca had one of those "this is it" moments one Halloween. "I bought a bunch of those break-the-glass-in-the-tube, glow-in-the-dark necklaces and we put them on our five dogs and played fetch with their lighted ball in the pitch black," she says. "Watching them run around, but only able to tell where they were by the lighted rings around their necks was hysterical. Really, it was. We were both laughing and I remember thinking, 'Yeah, I found the right guy.'"

And Rebecca feels the love when Ed makes her laugh at things that are out of her control. "I don't do out of my control well," she says. "One time after my diagnosis, but before my mastectomy, I said, 'I've decided I'm not going to have breast cancer anymore.' Without missing a beat and never bothering to look up from his computer, he said, 'Sure. Let's go with that.' I was stunned for a second, then burst out laughing. Which was exactly what I needed at that moment."

Hugs are good, too, Rebecca says. "But just from him. I don't really like it if others try to hug me."

Ed's into the hugs as well. "I've only just realized how important touch is to me," he says. "In two and a half years, we've never been apart more than twenty-four hours. Most evenings we sit in the living room, she at her art table, me at my laptop, sitting only six feet away from one another. I realized that something was bothering me and I said to her, 'I miss you,' but I didn't know what that meant exactly. After some serious thought, I realized that it meant being physically close, feeling her lie against me as we watch a movie, holding her in my arms after a long day."

Presumably they have since rectified that six-foot distance.

Brett's fiancée often leaves notes on his car windshield. "I love it!" he says. He likes cuddles on the couch, when she offers to pay for lunch or dinner, and when she finishes his crossword puzzles or buys him a book he might like. "I don't need much," he says. "I just need to know she thinks about me and understands me."

Joy loves feeling understood if she doesn't feel like going out or needs some solace. And she feels loved when she feels listened to. "As opposed to someone who is just waiting for me to stop talking so they can talk," she says.

And Nancy feels loved when her full-speed-ahead extrovert slows down for her. "When she gets pulled in a thousand different directions and I feel a little neglected, all it takes is for her to say, 'You are the most important thing in my life, period, nothing else,'" Nancy says. "She says, 'What do I need to do for you and what do I need to clear away?' and she does it. She takes care of my heart and that's what I need taken care of. There's very little else I need taken care of. I'm pretty self-sufficient."

I'm pretty self-sufficient, too—sometimes to my own detriment. It can be hard for me to admit I need anything from anyone, and if I fully indulge that, I'm pretty much guaranteed never to feel the love I need. That's a work in progress.

Like many women, however, I am attracted to a sense of humor, and my husband can make me laugh harder than anyone I've ever met. Once, not long ago, as I was wiping away tears of mirth after one of his bone-dry one-liners, he said, "I like making you laugh." And that made me feel loved.

What about you?

The Last Word
Is Never the Last Word

As I've said many times throughout this book (it's too important to say just once or twice or four hundred times), not only are introverts different from each other in many ways, we also are all so much more than our introversion and extroversion. Even if you consider just one theory of personality alone—the Big Five you heard about in college psych courses, for example—you have to factor in four other traits: neuroticism, agreeableness, conscientiousness, openness to experience. We are all different degrees of each of those.

Still, it's quite clear to me that many introverts take their introversion seriously as an important facet of who they are and how they interact with the world, in which case it certainly is a factor in what we need from our relationships, and how we keep those relationships healthy. And that's why I have taken the time to parse different ways that introversion works for and against us in our search for and success in love relationships.

I don't suggest finding your love match is easy. It's not. We all know that. It takes a lot of effort, a lot of time, probably some frog kissing. It requires self-knowledge, insight, compassion, a sense of humor, stepping out of your comfort zone, opening your mind, and some awkward conversation. There might be heartbreak along the way, which is one good reason to make sure you don't neglect your friends when you're newly in love; you might just need them later. And then once you've found love, you have all sorts of new challenges to take on as you negotiate time, space, emotional needs.

But what I hope this book will help you do is embark on your search for that special someone with a better idea of what it is you want and need from your relationship; of when you are and aren't being true to the introvert you are; of the best ways to ask for what you need—be it quiet time or a social director. I hope this book reassures you that there's nothing wrong with wanting both intimacy and personal space. The two are not mutually exclusive.

Once you've found your happily-ever-after partner, it's unlikely that you'll work out all the issues we discussed once and done. People change, circumstances change, you might find yourself re-negotiating time and time again over the course of a relationship. While introversion and extroversion are what personality psychologists consider "stable traits"—that is, they tend to remain stable over the course of your lifetime—and so you probably won't suddenly find yourself wanting to lead the conga line, you might find you need different things at different times. Maybe eking out alone time will be more important when you have kids in the house but less so when the nest is empty. Maybe shifts in your job circumstances will affect how you feel about socializing. Maybe you will simply change over time and find yourself wanting more interaction than you once did—or less. Maybe your partner will.

But once you have a grip on the basic personality differences behind conflicting needs, discussions should be less volatile and more productive. Once you both understand that different isn't better or worse but merely different, the things you don't agree on will seem less to portend incompatibility than to suggest compromise.

So whether you're looking for love or are already deep in the heart of it, I hope this book has provided helpful ways to think about your own style of introversion and how it fits into the relationship you want, or the relationship you have.

Further Reading About Relationships

Gary Chapman, *The Five Love Languages: The Secret to Love That Lasts* (Chicago: Northfield Publishing, 2009).

Helen Fisher, PhD, *Why Him? Why Her?: How to Find and Keep Lasting Love* (New York: Henry Holt, 2010).

John Gottman, PhD, with Nan Silver, *The Seven Principles for Making Marriage Work: A Practical Guide from the Country's Foremost Relationship Expert* (New York: Harmony, 2000).

Willard F. Harley Jr., *His Needs, Her Needs: Building an Affair-Proof Marriage* (Ada, Mich.: Revell/Baker Group, 2002).

Harville Hendrix, PhD, *Getting the Love You Want: A Guide for Couples*, rev. ed. (New York: Henry Holt, 2007).

Amir Levine, MD, and Rachel S. F. Heller, MA, *Attached: The New Science of Adult Attachment and How It Can Help You Find—and Keep—Love* (New York: Tarcher, 2012).

Acknowledgments

A huge and heartfelt thank you to my panel of introverts, who were thoughtful, responsive, funny, deep, candid, wise, and all-around swell. I could not have written this book without their generosity, and that's no exaggeration.

Equally heartfelt thanks to my agent, Penny Nelson, who took me on when I had hardly a clue (thank you, thank you); and my talented editor, Meg Leder, who can get me on the right track and out of a self-inflicted funk with just a few kind words.

Thanks to all my friends, who (whether they know it or not) pick me up when I'm down, particularly Karen Reiter, Joy Nelson, Diana Stewart, Lesley Gaspar, Dave Baumbach, Nancy Kruh, and Ashley Powell; and thanks to my brother, Nick Dembling, and my most excellent in-laws, Jo Ann and Tom Battles, whose enthusiasm and support do wonders for my motivation. Thanks to my husband, the other Tom Battles, because of everything; and to our dog, Jack, because he's a good boy.

Index